Herodotus
and the
Persian Wars

John Claughton

CAMBRIDGE
UNIVERSITY PRESS

CAMBRIDGE UNIVERSITY PRESS

Cambridge, New York, Melbourne, Madrid, Cape Town, Singapore, São Paulo, Delhi

Cambridge University Press
The Edinburgh Building, Cambridge CB2 8RU, UK

www.cambridge.org
Information on this title: www.cambridge.org/9780521689434

First published 2008

Printed in the United Kingdom at the University Press, Cambridge

A catalogue record for this publication is available from the British Library

ISBN   978-0-521-68943-4 paperback

ACKNOWLEDGEMENTS

We are grateful to the following for permission to reproduce copyright photographs:

akg-images/Erich Lessing: p.87; ancient-greece.org: p.40; The Art Archive/Alfredo
Dagli Orti: p.52; The Art Archive/Accademia Venice/Alfredo Dagli Orti: p.4; The
Art Archive/Gianni Dagli Orti: p.50; The Art Archive/Acropolis Museum Athens/
Gianni Dagli Orti: p.109; The Art Archive/Archaeological Museum Delphi/Gianni
Dagli Orti: p.12; The Art Archive/National Archaeological Museum Athens/Gianni
Dagli Orti: p.44; Borromeo/Art Resource, NY: p.100; Nimatallah/Art Resource, NY:
p.88; Vanni/Art Resource, NY: p.138; © Ashmolean Museum, University of Oxford,
UK/The Bridgeman Art Library: p.126; © Bisotun, Iran/Alinari/The Bridgeman Art
Library: p.76; Louvre, Paris, France/Giraudon/The Bridgeman Art Library: p.84;
Louvre, Paris, France/Peter Willi/The Bridgeman Art Library: p.16; © The Trustees
of the British Museum: pp.28, 31; Wolfgang Kaehler20_www.wkaehlerphoto.com,
photographersdirect.com: p.93; The Kobal Collection/Warner Bros/Legendary
Pictures: p.92; ©1990 Photo Scala, Florence: p.141; © 2003 Photo Scala, Florence: p.6;
© 1990 Photo Scala, Florence – courtesy of the Ministero Beni e Att. Culturali: p.45;
© 2003 AP/Topham: p.110.

Cover picture: Louvre, Paris, France/Giraudon/The Bridgeman Art Library.

Picture Research by Sandie Huskinson-Rolfe of PHOTOSEEKERS.

Contents

Preface

'The author is dead' is one of the truths of modern literary theory. That is certainly true of Herodotus, but not much else is equally secure. He came from Halicarnassus, in what was then Ionia and is now south-west Turkey. He tells us that in the very first words of his work and no one has doubted it. He also tells us that he went as far south as Elephantine in Egypt (2.29), as far north as the Black Sea (4.76–81) and as far west as Metapontum in southern Italy (4.15), although some people have doubted the reliability of these statements. The traditional date of his birth is 484 BC, and it is likely that this is not far wrong. It is clear that he was writing at some time between the 440s and 420s BC, but greater precision is impossible. It is very unlikely that there was any contemporary record of his career and what exists is merely the product of the imaginative use of what Herodotus himself wrote. No matter how far Herodotus travelled in his study of the world or when or where he wrote his work, one thing is true: he was not an eye-witness of the historic events which form the climax of his work, the Persian attack on Athens in 490 BC and the Persian invasion of Greece in 480/479 BC. His account of people and places and battles and events had to be made from the things that he saw and the stories that he was told.

The first great wonder of Greek literature is that its earliest works, the *Iliad* and *Odyssey* of Homer, should be so substantial, complex and sophisticated. However, Herodotus' work is its own wonder. Herodotus had antecedents in the recording of past events, but his achievement goes beyond that. Out of the innumerable fragments of evidence he makes a narrative that is both infinitely rich and structurally coherent. The author has two remarkable qualities: he has the humanity to be interested in and value all that he comes to know and he has the intelligence to create a structure that answers the fundamental question of why the Greeks and the Persians came to fight each other. That answer is not a simple one; it encompasses the will of the gods and the necessity of fate, the character of men and the role of chance, revenge and retribution, the characteristics of a country and the impact it has on its people. And it is the structure of causation that forms the narrative: events and stories are placed because they explain and relate to each other.

Herodotus' work, like Homer's, is complex and sophisticated but it has not always had that reputation. Set against the apparently icy objectivity of Thucydides, the other great historian of the fifth century BC, it was seen as a succession of travellers' tales or good anecdotes told by an unreliable and naive narrator. That is no longer so and Herodotus has been rehabilitated, not least through the production of really good commentaries of key books in recent years. There is now a much greater understanding that Herodotus is conveying, in the way he knew best, key truths and fundamental issues about human existence.

This book has five specific aims. The first is to make some of the key passages of Herodotus accessible to an audience that might be daunted by 500 pages of translation. To achieve that accessibility, the translation strives to capture the relaxed, story-telling style of Herodotus, the notes answer questions which an inquisitive reader might want answered and the questions are there to make the reader think beyond the translation. The second aim is to show how Herodotus is exploring in his own way – which may not be the modern way of history – complex issues of causation – that is, to bring out what Herodotus is showing rather than telling. The third purpose is to lead the reader from the passages that are in this book back to other passages in Herodotus that are not.* There is another volume out there waiting to be written with the bits that I have excluded. The fourth aim is to encourage the reader to think about the world that Herodotus describes, a world that has human beings who are such as we are, but also another country, another world, where things are different. And the final aim is to make us contemplate the similarities between the world he describes and our world: it was not only in 480 BC that East and West faced each other.

Writing this book has brought me great personal enjoyment; the more I have studied Herodotus to produce this book, the more I have come to appreciate the true wonder of his work. I would like to thank, in particular, James Morwood for enhancing that enjoyment by being an editor of great patience, but even greater encouragement, and Angus Bowie for generously making available his *Book VIII* of the *Histories* before publication. I would like to dedicate this book to Tom Braun, my undergraduate tutor who taught me Herodotus. He showed me what it meant to love learning and that the life of the mind is the only life worth living.

---

* In the notes, references to Herodotus' work are given *with* page numbers if the passage referred to is translated in this volume; *without* page numbers if it is not translated here.

Timeline

All dates are BC.

3000–1450	Minoan Civilization on Crete
2700–1100	Egypt: Old, Middle and New Kingdoms
1600–1200	Mycenaean Civilization
c. 1200	The Fall of Troy
1100–700	'Dark Ages' in Greece
1050–950	Migration of Ionian Greeks from mainland Greece to Ionia and the islands of the Aegean
776	Founding of Olympic Games
753	Foundation of Rome
750	Introduction of Greek alphabet, adapted from the Phoenicians
750–700	Homer and Hesiod
c. 680–652	Gyges, king of Lydia
594	Solon, archon at Athens
560–546	Croesus, king of Lydia
559–530	Cyrus, king of Persia
550	Cyrus' defeat of Astyages, king of Media
546	Cyrus' defeat of Croesus and conquest of Lydia
546–510	Rule of Pisistratus and Hippias as tyrants in Athens
530–522	Cambyses, king of Persia
522–486	Darius, king of Persia
508	Democratic reforms of Cleisthenes at Athens
499–494	Ionian revolt
490	Persian attack on Greece: battle of Marathon
486	Accession of Xerxes as king of Persia
c. 484	Birth of Herodotus
480–479	Persian invasion of Greece: Thermopylae, Salamis, Plataea
472	Aeschylus' *Persians*
447–432	Building of the Parthenon in Athens
431–404	Peloponnesian War: Athens against Sparta
404	Defeat of Athens
356–323	Alexander the Great

1 Introduction and the kidnapping of women

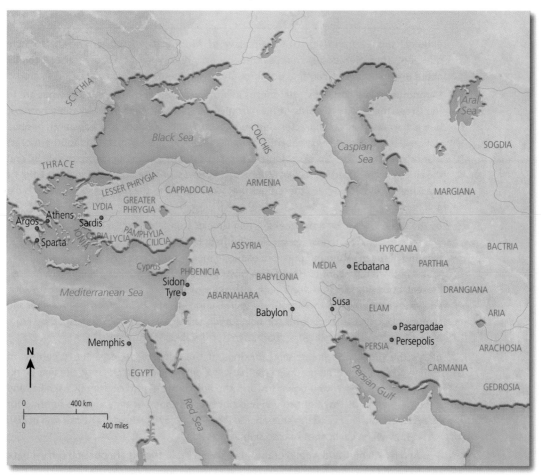

The Persian empire and neighbouring territories in the fifth century BC.

Although Herodotus' work culminates in the great battles of 490 BC and 480–479 BC, his work is remarkable in its range. He begins with the world of myth and travels through many places and over generations in time to explore the relations between the Greeks and the Persians.

Introduction

This is the presentation of the **enquiry** of **Herodotus of Halicarnassus**. The purpose of this work is to ensure that the actions of mankind are not rubbed out by time, and that great and wondrous deeds, some performed **by the Greeks, some by non-Greeks**, are not without due **glory**. In particular, the purpose is to explain **why** they waged war against each other.

5

---

enquiry this is a translation of the Greek word, *historie*: its related verb means 'to ask a question'. Thus, Herodotus' work is not necessarily history in our narrow sense. It can be about anything that he can find out through asking questions.

Herodotus of Halicarnassus Herodotus identifies himself and his origins in what are in the Greek the first two words of his narrative. He is no impersonal or invisible narrator but a narrator whose character and judgements and opinions are constantly visible. Halicarnassus is one of the great cities of Ionia, modern-day Bodrum on the southern coast of modern Turkey. The Greeks colonized the east coast of the Aegean around 1000 BC and the cities they founded there, like Miletus and Ephesus, became some of the great cities of the Greek world. It was also these cities that were closest to the non-Greek world of Lydia and Persia.

by the Greeks, some by non-Greeks 'non-Greeks' translates the Greek word *barbaroi*. It was used to describe non-Greek speakers perhaps because their language sounded like the bleating of sheep. Although the word comes to mean barbarian in our sense of uncivilized, that is not what it meant to Herodotus. One of his great strengths is that his account does present both sides of the world and both sides of the war. Indeed, there is more time and space given over to the non-Greek world, and Plutarch, a Greek writer of the second century AD, criticizes Herodotus for being *philobarbaros*, a lover of the barbarian. From now on *barbaros* is translated as 'barbarian' for the sake of simplicity.

glory the Greeks are immensely conscious of the need to preserve the greatness of human achievement. The purpose goes back to Homer's *Iliad* and *Odyssey*, the first works of Greek literature, written down towards the end of the eighth century BC. Achilles and the other heroes at Troy fight to win and fight for honour, but they are also fighting for glory (*kleos*), the chance to be remembered long after they are dead. As Hector says in *Iliad* 7.81–91, when he challenges Ajax to single combat:

> And if I kill him, and Apollo grants my prayer, I shall strip his armour and carry it back to sacred Ilios, and hang it in dedication at the temple of Apollo the far-shooter, but his body I shall return to the well-benched ships, so that the long-haired Achaians can give the rites of burial and heap a mound for him by the broad Hellespont.
> And people will say, even men of generations not yet born, as they sail by over the sparkling sea in their many-benched ships: 'This is the mound of a man who died long ago. He was the greatest of men, and glorious Hektor killed him.' This is what they will say: and my glory will never die.
>
> Translation by J. M. Hammond

why perhaps this word represents the beginning of the writing of history as we conceive it. Events can be remembered and recorded, but Herodotus brings the purpose of explaining the causes of events. Although his approach to narrative is often through the telling of stories rather than specific analysis, the stories are his way of exploring causation.

The kidnapping of women 1.1–5

1.1   **Learned Persians** say that the **Phoenicians** were responsible for the falling out. Their account is that the Phoenicians came **to this sea** from what is called the Red Sea and settled in the land that they occupy to this day. They undertook great sea voyages, carrying cargo from **Egypt and Assyria.** They visited other countries and they also came to **Argos.** At this time Argos was pre-eminent amongst all the cities 5 in the land which is now called Greece. When the Phoenicians got to Argos, they laid out their goods for sale. On the fifth or sixth day after their arrival, when they had sold almost everything, lots of women came down to the shore, including the king's daughter. Her name – and the Greeks agree on this – was **Io**, the daughter

---

Learned Persians   Herodotus begins with the world of myth, which was central to the minds of the ancient Greeks. This is not, in itself, an unexpected place to start. However, it is strange that Herodotus should start, and largely stay, with what he claims to be a Persian account of Greek myth. It is also strange that these myths, normally full of wonders and metamorphosis, should be told in a deliberately realistic way. All of this narrative is presented in indirect speech, making it clear that it is meant to be the Persian account: it is specifically not Herodotus'. Despite making the stories seem realistic, Herodotus does refer obliquely to the better-known versions of the stories: the Greek reader would know what he meant.

Phoenicians   the Phoenicians occupied the land which is now part of Syria and Lebanon: their two great ports were Tyre and Sidon. They were the great seafarers and traders of the eastern Mediterranean who also founded colonies in the western Mediterranean, Carthage and Cadiz. The Greeks' great debt to the Phoenicians was their alphabet; the Greeks adapted it towards the end of the eighth century BC, when they came into contact with them through trade. See 5.58 for Herodotus' account of the Greeks' taking of the Phoenician alphabet.

to this sea   Herodotus means the Mediterranean: the Greeks not only occupied mainland Greece, the islands of the Aegean and Ionia, but also sent out colonies to Sicily, southern Italy and beyond.

Egypt and Assyria   these were the two great and prosperous empires of the time before the Persian empire. The location of Phoenicia meant that the Phoenicians were ideally placed to transport the goods of these two largely land-locked countries.

Argos   a city-state in the north-east of the Peloponnese. In the Mycenaean age (1600–1200 BC) it had been a major city: one of the most common names for the Greeks in the *Iliad* is 'Argives'.

Io   any Greek would know the myth of Io; she was the priestess of Hera at Argos, but was seduced by Zeus. She was transformed into a white cow, either by Zeus or by Hera, and was watched over by the monster Argos. Hermes killed Argos, but Io was driven mad by a gadfly sent by Hera and she wandered the earth until finally she came to Egypt. There she was restored by Zeus to her human form and gave birth to Epaphus, the ancestor of Danaus. Danaus later returned to Argos to become king. The Greek myth has nothing quite so commonplace as Phoenician traders stealing local girls.

---

of Inachus. Well, they were all standing around by the sterns and buying the goods 10
that most appealed to them, and then the Phoenicians gave the word and went for
them. Most of the women got away but Io and some others were captured. The
Phoenicians put them onto their ships and sailed away back to Egypt.

1.2   This is the Persians' account of how Io came to Egypt – **although the Greeks
don't agree** – and they say that this was the beginning of the acts of injustice. 15
They go on to say that, after this, some Greeks – they can't give any name to them
– came to Tyre in Phoenicia and seized **Europa**, the daughter of the king. These

The Rape of Europa, *by the eighteenth-century Italian artist Francesco Zuccarelli. The
traditional story of Zeus tricking Europa in the shape of a bull and carrying her off to Crete was
a very popular subject for artists from the sixth century BC onwards. This painting conveys the
misplaced delight of Europa and her friends as she sets forth with Zeus.*

although the Greeks don't agree   Herodotus knowingly nods at the rich Greek version
of the myth described in the previous note.

Europa   the daughter of the king of Phoenicia. Zeus fell in love with her as she played
on the seashore. He turned himself into a beautiful bull and enticed her by his mildness
to get onto his back. The bull then plunged into the sea and swam to Crete. Europa
bore Zeus two or three sons: Minos, the king of Crete and keeper of the Minotaur;
Rhadamanthys, who became a judge in the underworld; and Sarpedon, a hero at Troy.
In 4.46 Herodotus questions whether Europe could be named after Europa, not least
because she never visited Europe.

would have been **Cretans.** They reckon that this was tit for tat, but it was hereafter the Greeks who were responsible for the second crime. For they sailed in a warship to **Aea** in Colchis and the river Phasis and then, when they had done **all that they had come to do**, they seized **Medea**, the daughter of the king. The king of Colchis sent a messenger to Greece and demanded **retribution for the kidnap**, asking for the return of his daughter. The **Greeks' reply** was that, since they hadn't given any retribution for the kidnap of Io, they couldn't see why they should give them any. 20

1.3 In the **next generation** after this **Alexander**, the son of Priam, who had heard all of these stories, wanted to get a wife from Greece by kidnapping; he knew very well that he wouldn't face any punishment, since everyone else had got away with it. So he kidnapped Helen and the Greeks decided to send messengers to ask for the return of Helen and demand retribution for the kidnap. When they produced this 25

Cretans as in the story of Io, Herodotus hints at the accepted Greek version of the myth by referring obliquely to the destination of the bull.

Aea on the eastern coast of the Black Sea, a very long way from Phoenicia and Argos.

all that they had come to do Herodotus suppresses the mythical part of the story, described in the note below.

Medea Jason and the Argonauts set forth to Colchis to steal the Golden Fleece. Medea, the daughter of Aeëtes, the king of Colchis, fell in love with Jason and then helped him to kill the fire-breathing dragon that guarded the Golden Fleece. With Jason she left her father and home and slowed down her pursuers by cutting her brother into pieces and throwing the bits into the sea.

retribution for the kidnap Herodotus creates a pattern in his narrative by repetition of the words for retribution and kidnap. The first of these two words is critical to the whole of Herodotus' history. There is a pattern in events of repayment: men repay men for the deeds they do and the gods also pay men back for what they have done. As W. H. Auden wrote in his poem *September 1, 1939*, 'Those to whom evil is done, Do evil in return.'

Greeks' reply Herodotus makes a link between the stories by making the Greeks refer to the previous kidnap to justify their action. Such joining of usually separate myths to create a causal link is unexpected. In the usual version, Medea wasn't kidnapped; she chose to go with Jason.

next generation Greek myth doesn't really have a strict chronology, but there is a sense that it comes in two generations; the sons of the men who accompanied Jason on the *Argo* were the heroes of the Trojan War. Even so, Herodotus is once again making the mythological age sound like historical time.

Alexander the alternative name for Paris, the son of King Priam and the brother of Hector. Like the Argonauts, Paris and the Trojans see themselves as part of this sequence of kidnaps, and base their actions on previous events. As far as we know, this creation of the link is the invention of Herodotus.

argument, **the other side referred** to the kidnapping of Medea; since they hadn't 30
made any retribution or even given the girl back when they were asked, how could
they come wanting retribution from others? That was their argument.

1.4 Until this point it had just been a matter of kidnapping from each other, but
now the Greeks were very much to blame. For they were the first to launch an
invasion against Asia, rather than the other way about. The barbarians reckoned 35
that stealing women was an act of injustice, but **it was silly to make too much of a
fuss** about getting retribution for kidnapped women. It was only sensible to treat
it as of no account; it's obvious that, if a woman didn't want to get kidnapped, it
wouldn't happen. The Persians say that, when the women were being kidnapped,
the Asians didn't consider it important, but it was the Greeks who, for the sake 40
of a Spartan woman, gathered together a great expedition, went to Asia and
destroyed the power of Priam. For that reason **they have always considered the
Greeks to be their enemy. For the Persians claim Asia and the barbarian tribes
that live there as their own, whereas they consider that Europe and Greece are
something separate.** 45

*The abduction of
Helen is depicted here
on an Etruscan urn.
For more on Helen, see
the Oxford Classical
Dictionary.*

---

the other side referred once again Herodotus makes a link in the narrative between his
stories. It is not likely that the Trojans referred to Jason and Medea in their negotiations
over Helen.

it was silly to make too much of a fuss the use to which Herodotus puts myth is very
striking here. The tone of this account is very worldly and cynical.

they have always considered the Greeks to be their enemy underlying Herodotus'
telling of these myths is the sense that there has been long-standing division, enmity and
distrust between East and West. Whatever the reality of the stories told here, the two
worlds have always been enemies and that lives on in the fifth century.

For the Persians claim Asia ... something separate Herodotus returns to this theme at
the end of his narrative (see 9.116, p. 143).

1.5   This is the Persians' account of events and their conclusion is that the fall of Troy was the beginning of the enmity with the Greeks. The **Phoenicians**, however, do not agree with the Persians about Io. They say that they didn't have to kidnap her to bring her to Egypt. Rather, she had slept with the ship's captain in Argos and, when she realized that she was pregnant, she was too ashamed to tell her parents. 50 So she sailed willingly with the Phoenicians to avoid getting found out.

Now that is what the Persians and the Phoenicians say, but **I am not going to say** whether things happened this way or that way. I am going to start with the first person whom I myself know to have started acts of injustice towards the Greeks. I will then proceed in my account, dealing with **small cities as much as great cities**. 55 For of the cities that were great in the past, many of them are now small, and cities that are great in my time were small before. I know that **human happiness does not stay for long in the same place**, so I will make mention of both equally.

The purpose of history

At the very beginning of his work, Herodotus gives a very clear account of his purpose in writing. It is worth comparing similar statements made by other Greek and Roman historians, to see not only how purposes can differ, but also how the difference in purpose affects the difference in content and approach. In the two accounts given here, Thucydides was writing between 431 and at least 404 BC; and Livy lived between *c.* 57 BC and AD 17.

Perhaps my work will seem less pleasurable to hear because it lacks the element of story-telling. However, if all those who wish to see clearly what has happened – and what is likely to happen again in the future in the same or similar way, since that is human nature – judge my work to be useful, that will be enough for me. This work is laid down to be a possession for all time rather than a performance for an immediate audience.

Thucydides, *A History of the Peloponnesian War* 1.22

Phoenicians   once again Herodotus presents this rationalization and normalization of Greek myth.

I am not going to say   after giving this version of events, an attempt to make history out of myth, Herodotus does not give it any authorial support. He starts with things that he knows. His way, following his own enquiries, will be different and better.

small cities as much as great cities, human happiness does not stay for long in the same place   this is fundamental to Herodotus and secures his greatness. His work is about the fragility of humanity and success, and that very fragility is the reason why things, even obscure things in obscure places, need recording. Who is to know what will happen in the future? Even the Tin Islands (see 3.115, p. 37) might become the centre of the world at some point in history. The richness of Herodotus' narrative springs from his fundamental view of the world.

For my part, I would urge each of you to turn your attention to these issues: how they lived their lives, and what sort of men and what sort of skills it took to bring to birth and then increase this empire, both at home and on military campaign. Then each of you should follow in your minds how, as traditional teaching gradually slipped away, morality first became unsteady and then began more and more to decline so that in the end it totally collapsed. Now we have come to a time when we can endure neither our vices nor their remedies.

In your consideration of this story, there is one thing that is especially beneficial and fruitful, and that is to gaze upon the evidence of every example of behaviour, gathered together as if on a shining monument. There you will find things to be imitated by you and your city, and things, foul through and through, to be avoided. For either the love of the task which I have undertaken has deceived me or there has never been a city greater nor more devoted to the gods, nor richer in good models of behaviour, nor any city to which greed and extravagance have come so late, nor where so much honour has been given for so long to thrift and moderation.

Livy, *History of Rome*, Preface 9–11

1   What is Herodotus' purpose? What impact is that likely to have on the things that he might include?

2   What has Herodotus done to the stories that he tells? What does he introduce? What does he omit? How does he join them up?

3   At the end of his narrative, Herodotus does not vouch for the truth of all these stories. In that case, why does he bother telling them at all?

4   Are the stories of rape and kidnap funny? If so, how and why?

5   How does Herodotus' purpose differ from the purposes of Thucydides and Livy? What other reasons are there for writing history?

2 Croesus, the king of Lydia

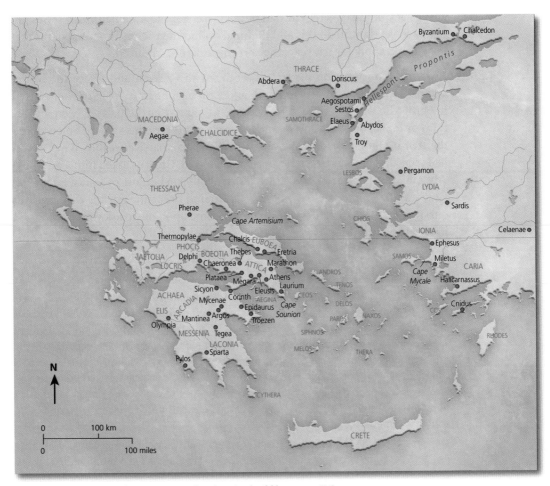

Greek city-states and regions in the fifth century BC.

Herodotus says that he will start with the first barbarian who performed acts of injustice against the Greeks: Croesus, who ruled over Lydia from 560 BC to 546 BC. He was the first Eastern king to subdue Greek-speaking people and form alliances with them. However, for reasons that will become obvious (see 1.91, pp. 19–20), Herodotus starts with how Gyges, Croesus' ancestor, came to power in *c.* 680 BC. He did so by murdering the king, Candaules, in a plot with Candaules' wife (1.6–12).

Croesus and Solon: 1.29–34

1.29   When **Sardis** was at the height of its wealth, all the wise men of Greece of that time came to visit the city at different times. The most famous of these was **Solon** the Athenian. At the Athenians' request, Solon had introduced a **law code** for them and, having done so, he went abroad for ten years. The **reason he gave for his travels was to see the world**, but, in fact, he had done it to avoid having to 5 change any of the laws that he had put in place. For the Athenians themselves did not have the right to do this and they had bound themselves by strong oaths that they would apply for ten years the laws that Solon introduced.

1.30   Anyway, Solon went on his travels, both for this reason and to see the world, and he went to see **Amasis** in Egypt and Croesus in Sardis. When Solon arrived 10 in Sardis, he was entertained by Croesus as a guest in the palace. Then, on the third or fourth day, on Croesus' orders, some of his servants showed Solon round the treasure houses and displayed all of Croesus' massive wealth. When Solon had seen all there was to see as far as time allowed, Croesus asked him a question: '**My Athenian friend**, we have heard much about you because of your wisdom and 15 your travels. People say that you have journeyed over much of the earth in your quest for knowledge. And so the desire has come upon me to ask you whether you have yet seen the happiest man in the world.'

Sardis   the capital of Lydia, 50 miles from the coast of the Aegean.

Solon, law code   Solon was *archon* (chief magistrate) in Athens in 594/3 BC and he was regarded by the Athenians as one of their greatest figures. His reforms involved changes in the relation of the workers to the owners of the land, the introduction of standard weights, measures and coinage, the re-organization of the Athenian citizen body to break the monopoly of the noble families, changes to the law system and the creation of a council of 400. His poetry, of which some substantial passages have survived, suggests that Solon was trying to achieve a compromise between the rich and poor. In later years it came to be seen as a step towards the democracy that was introduced by Cleisthenes in 508 BC and he was presented as a hero of the democracy.

The date of Solon's reforms does create some difficulty: if he is on his travels soon after 594/3 BC, he could not have met Croesus, who wasn't king of Lydia for another 30 years. One possibility is that Solon did not introduce his reforms in 594/3 BC, but 20 years later, which would at least allow the possibility that Solon and Croesus could have met.

reason he gave for his travels was to see the world   Herodotus might want us to see the similarity between himself and Solon, the travelling wise man.

Amasis   became pharaoh in 570 BC and, in the face of Persian expansion, formed links with a range of states, Lydia, Samos and Cyrene. His reign, which lasted for over forty years, was seen as a period of great peace and prosperity in Egypt (see 2.172–82).

My Athenian friend   the friendly tone between the two men is striking and the word for 'friend', *xenos*, opens a continuing theme in the work, the role of guest-friendship. These words recur at the very end of Herodotus' work as Artayctes recognizes the truth of an omen (9.120, pp. 144–5).

Croesus asked this **question** in the expectation that he was that happiest man. Solon, however, **didn't flatter him and told him the truth.** He said, 'Tellos the Athenian, your majesty.' Now Croesus was amazed at what he said and he asked another question rather more urgently, 'What ever makes you think that Tellos is the happiest?' And Solon said, 'Tellos lived in a prosperous city. He had fine children. He saw children born to all these children and they all survived. He was prosperous, in our terms anyway, and he had a most glorious end to his life. In a battle between the Athenians and their neighbours at **Eleusis**, Tellos came to the aid of his own side, routed the enemy and died the finest of deaths. The Athenians gave him a **state burial at the very place where he fell** and did him great honour.'

1.31   Solon's story of Tellos, with all its talk of happiness, led Croesus on to ask to whom he would give second place after Tellos. He thought that he would at least get second prize. Solon said, '**Cleobis and Biton**. They were from the city of **Argos**. They had enough to live on and, in addition, were physically strong, as this story will show. They were both **prize-winning athletes** and the following story is

---

question   Herodotus' whole narrative is full of leaders asking questions. How good they are at listening or how they react to the answer is a recurrent theme.

didn't flatter him and told him the truth   Herodotus' narrative continually deals with the issue of advice. In some cases, the situation or the person does not allow the chance for genuine advice to be given. In others, good advice is given and ignored.

Tellos   Solon's answer is wondrously abrupt and wholly unexpected, especially for Croesus. In the Greek it is emphasized by the brevity of the answer. This is Tellos' one moment in history, a man who embodies much that is Greek, as the whole work will show. It is important to think about the exact details that Solon considers to be central to a happy life. This battle between Athens and her neighbour is otherwise unknown and cannot be securely dated.

Eleusis   a town that overlooks the bay of Salamis (see map on p. 108), where the Eleusinian Mysteries were held. Eleusis and the Mysteries reappear immediately before the battle of Salamis (8.65 and note, pp. 102–3). The ancient site of the Mysteries is now hemmed in by oil refineries.

state burial at the very place where he fell   this can be compared with the honour done to the Athenians who died at Marathon in 490 BC, or the Spartans at Thermopylae in 480 BC (7.228, pp. 94–5).

Cleobis and Biton   an odd couple to mention. No other source before Herodotus tells their story.

Argos   Argos may have been a place famous to the Greeks (see note on 1.1), but it would have meant nothing to Croesus. Nor would he have been particularly impressed by talk of oxen late back from the fields.

prize-winning athletes   the Greeks were deeply interested in physical prowess and athletic competition. Not only were there major games at Olympia, but also at Delphi, Nemea and Corinth.

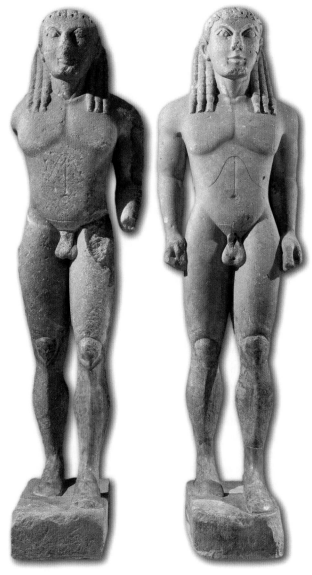

told about them. There was a festival in Argos in honour of the goddess **Hera**, and it was absolutely essential that their mother should travel to the temple in an ox-cart. However, the oxen didn't turn up from the fields in time. Because of the shortage of time, the young men had to go under the yoke themselves and pull the cart. Their mother rode on the cart and they pulled it 45 **stades** to the temple. And when they had done this under the gaze of the whole people, there came to them the best possible end of their lives, an end through which god showed that **it is better for man to be dead than to go on living**. All the men of Argos were standing around, praising the strength of the young men, whilst all the women of Argos were praising the mother who had produced such fine children. Their mother was overjoyed at what they had done and the **reputation** they had won. Standing in front of the statue of the goddess, she prayed that the goddess should give to

These two statues, named on their bases as Cleobis and Biton, were found in 1893 and now stand in the Delphi Museum. They are dated c. 600–580 BC and came from Argos. They stand 2.35 metres tall and in their massive muscularity they are typical of the male sculpture of this period.

Hera   the wife of Zeus and the patron goddess of Argos. For her love of Argos, see Homer *Iliad* 4.51–2.

stades   a stade is *c.* 200 yards, the length of a stadium and hence the length of a race. 45 stades is just over 5 miles.

it is better for man to be dead than to go on living   this is a common Greek attitude, reflecting their sense of the fragility of human life.

reputation   the mother of Cleobis and Biton is as concerned about glory as Hector in the *Iliad* (see note on the Introduction, p. 2).

her sons, Cleobis and Biton, who had done her such honour, whatever was best for 60 a man to receive. And after this prayer and the sacrifices and the feasting, the young men lay down to sleep in the temple itself and never woke up again. That was their end. The people of Argos made statues of them and set them up at **Delphi** to commemorate the best of men.'

1.32 And so Solon gave the second prize for happiness to these two. Croesus exploded 65 and said: 'My Athenian friend, is my happiness worth absolutely nothing? Do you really think that I am not the equal even of ordinary people?' And Solon said, 'Croesus, you ask a question about human life of a man who knows that **god is envious and causes trouble.** In a long life we see and suffer many things that we would rather not. I set the limit of human life at **70 years.** Seventy years contain 70 **25,200 days,** if we don't include **intercalated months.** If we want to make alternate years longer by a month so that the seasons come round at due time, there would be 35 extra months in seventy years. That's another 1,050 days. So, in 70 years, there are, in total, **26,250 days,** and each one of those days brings in something completely different from the next. And so, Croesus, **man is all chance.** To me you 75

Delphi   see note on Apollo at 1.87.

god is envious and causes trouble   the Judaeo-Christian tradition may have a god of justice and love, but not all gods have to be that way. For the Greeks the gods were powerful, but not necessarily just. Solon expresses a common Greek judgement that the gods resent human success and strive to keep humans in their place. Solon goes on to say that they also just like causing trouble. During the narrative we are led to consider whether the gods do behave in this way.

70 years, 25,200 days, 26,250 days   Solon here echoes the scientific enquiry that was an important part of the Greeks' progress in the sixth century BC. Men like Thales, Anaximander and Anaximenes were enquiring into the natural world and trying to answer fundamental questions of a scientific and philosophical nature. So Solon offers both mathematics and astronomy in the form of his account of the length of a man's life, and metaphysics in the consideration of the nature of a man's lot and linguistic philosophy in his consideration of the meanings of words.

One of the most accessible routes to these authors is through *Early Greek Philosophy,* edited by Jonathan Barnes (see Recommended reading).

intercalated months   intercalated months are inserted into the calendar to ensure that there is a match between the lunar year (12 months of 30 days) and the solar year (365 days). Solon's calculation doesn't work because he is inserting too many days; he would end up with a year of 375 days.

man is all chance   Solon's account of human fragility can be matched in other works of Greek literature, but particularly tragedy. For example, the fate of Oedipus as told by Sophocles in *Oedipus the King* enacts the fall from honour to disgrace. Indeed, the whole of Herodotus' narrative of the war explores the role of forces beyond human control or understanding. Once again, we take with us into Herodotus' narrative Solon's judgement on human existence. We are asked to consider whether Solon is right. Or perhaps Herodotus is wiser than this wise man and it is not only chance at work.

seem to be very wealthy and to be the king of many people. But I cannot yet give you an answer to your question until I know that your life has come to a good end. A man of great wealth is no happier than a man who only has enough for the day, unless good fortune and prosperity attend him to the end of his life. For there are many very wealthy people who are unhappy, and many with just enough 80 who are happy. The man of great wealth but no happiness has the advantage over the man of good fortune in only two respects, but the man of good fortune has many advantages over the wealthy but unfortunate man. The rich man has more opportunity to fulfil his desires and to bear any great disaster that might befall him. The poor man, however, has the following advantages. He may not have 85 the same ability to cope with disaster and desire, but his good fortune protects him from them. He lives without disability or disease or misfortune, and he is fortunate in his children and in his physical appearance. And if, in addition to all of this, he will end his life well, that man is the one whom you seek, the one worthy to be called happy. Before a man dies you should refrain from calling him 90 happy: he is only lucky.

'It is just not possible for **a single human being to have everything, just as no country produces everything so that it is self-sufficient**: it has one thing, but lacks something else. The country with the most good things is the best. In the same way, no single human body has everything. It has some things, but lacks 95 others. Whoever continues to have most things and then comes to the end of his life in good fortune, that man, your majesty, deserves in my opinion to be called happy. We must in all things look to the end, to how things will turn out. **For God has given many people wealth and then has destroyed them utterly.'**

1.33 Croesus didn't like what Solon had to say, so he sent him away, paying him no 100 regard. He thought that Solon had to be very stupid to tell him to discount his present prosperity and look to the end of everything.

1.34 After Solon left, god took from Croesus a terrible revenge because, as you might guess, he thought that he was the happiest of all men.

---

a single human being to have everything   in the final book of the *Iliad* (24.527–34) Achilles makes a similar statement, saying that no human gets only good in his life: the best one can expect is a mixture of good and evil.

just as no country produces everything so that it is self-sufficient   see 3.106 (p. 35) for Herodotus' account of the diversity of the world.

For God ... destroyed them utterly   Solon's account of human existence here reflects traditional Greek ideas of the time: the gods focus their attention on those with excessive wealth and bring them back down to size. For a particularly vivid example, see the story of Polycrates of Samos (3.39–43) and Artabanus' judgement of events (7.10e, p. 57).

God's revenge took both a public and private form. Croesus had two sons: one, Atys, the finest of young men, the other deaf and dumb from birth. Croesus was warned in a dream that Atys would be killed by a spear-point, so he kept him from all danger. In the end he was persuaded to allow him to go hunting. Whilst he was hunting, he was inadvertently killed by Adrastus, a man whom Croesus had taken into his own home after he had killed his own brother. Adrastus, overwhelmed by grief at what he had done, killed himself over the tomb of Atys (1.34–45).

The fall of Croesus: 1.86–91

Two years later Croesus decided to face the growing power of Persia by attacking Cyrus, the king of Persia, who had recently conquered the **Medes**. Before he did so, he tested out a number of oracles and, on the basis of Delphi's capacity to solve his riddles, he put his trust in the oracle there. When he consulted Delphi, the oracle told him that, if he attacked the **Persians**, he would destroy a great empire. He failed to understand the enigmatic nature of the responses and was encouraged, wrongly, in his attack on the Persian empire. Croesus was defeated in battle and Sardis was captured and sacked. At that moment, when Croesus was about to be killed by a Persian soldier, Croesus' second son recovered his speech to save his life (1.46–56, 75–85).

1.86 And so the Persians took Sardis and captured Croesus himself. He had ruled for fourteen years and the siege had lasted fourteen days. As the prophecy had said, he did destroy a great empire – his own. When the Persians had captured Croesus, they brought him to Cyrus who put him on a pyre with fourteen Lydian children. Perhaps Cyrus' purpose was to make a victory offering to some god, perhaps it was to fulfil a vow, perhaps, being aware that Croesus was a god-fearing man, 5

Medes an Indo-European tribe who occupied the land to the south-west of the Caspian Sea. In the late sixth century BC they grew in power and conquered Assyria, sacking Nimrud and Nineveh: some of this is recounted by Herodotus (1.95–103). This expansion brought the Medes into contact with Lydia, and Herodotus recounts a battle of 585 BC between the two peoples brought to an end by an eclipse (1.74).

Persians a people who occupied land south of Media, to the east of the Persian Gulf. In 550 BC the Median king, Astyages, was deposed by Cyrus, the king of Persia (1.123–30). According to Herodotus, Cyrus was the child of the daughter of Astyages and a Median nobleman. The story of Cyrus' birth, miraculous upbringing and overthrow of Astyages is told in 1.107–30. The Persians also conquered Babylonia and Media, becoming the dominant people of the region and building three great palaces at Persepolis, Pasargadae and Susa. They maintained their empire in the area until the arrival of Alexander the Great.

he put him on the pyre wanting to know if some god might intervene to protect him from being burnt alive.

Whatever the reason, **the story is told** that Cyrus did this, and, as Croesus stood on the pyre, it came into his mind, even in such a dreadful situation, that the words of Solon, that no living man could be called happy, were divinely inspired. And when this thought came to him, he heaved a great sigh, groaned and, in the midst of the silence, he called out 'Solon' three times. When Cyrus heard this, he ordered his interpreters to ask Croesus whom he was calling, and they went and asked. At first, Croesus remained silent and didn't answer the question but then, when he was forced to do so, he spoke.

This red-figure amphora was painted by Myson in about 500–490 BC. It was found in an Etruscan tomb at Vulci in Italy. It is unique in representing a specific historic event: Croesus, who is named on the vase, is seated in royal splendour and pours a libation onto the pyre while an attendant, named as Eutymos, starts the fire.

he put him on the pyre   Herodotus' uncertainty about Cyrus' motive is reflected in other versions of the story: see the vase painting and the version of the poet Bacchylides (p. 21).

the story is told   Herodotus usually narrates stories directly in his own voice. Sometimes, when he does not want to lend his own authorial voice to the narrative, he tells it in the syntactical form of indirect speech. That is what he does here. It is worth asking why he changes at this moment.

'What I would want most of all is that every king should talk to this man.' Since they didn't understand what he meant, they asked him again. As the bystanders urged him to speak and were making a great uproar, he said: 'Solon the Athenian came to my kingdom and, when he had seen all my prosperity, he rubbished it, or 20 words to that effect. Everything has turned out for me as he said. His words were not directed only at me, but at all of mankind, and especially those who think that they are happy.'

As Croesus was explaining this, the edges of the pyre, which had already been lit, began to burn. Cyrus, when he heard from the interpreters what Croesus said, 25 had a change of heart. He realized that he, a human being, was committing to the fire another human being who had been no less in good fortune than he was. Furthermore, he feared that there may be some **retribution** for his actions and he reasoned that **nothing in human life was safe**. He gave the order, therefore, that the pyre should be put out at once and that Croesus and those with him should 30 be brought down from the pyre. But, when they tried, they could not bring the fire under control.

1.87   At this point, the following happened, according to the Lydians. When Croesus saw everyone trying to put out the fire, he realized that Cyrus had changed his mind. When they couldn't do it, he shouted out to **Apollo**, '**If any of my gifts** has 35 pleased you, stand by me and protect me from this present danger.' He made this plea in tears and suddenly, from a clear sky and a perfect calm, clouds gathered and a storm crashed down. There was a torrential downpour and the fire was put out. In this way Cyrus learnt that Croesus truly was a man dear to the gods and a good man. When he had brought him down from the pyre, he asked the following 40 question, 'Croesus, who persuaded you to invade my country and to make me your enemy rather than your friend?'

---

retribution   as in the narrative of the kidnapping of women, Herodotus sees retribution at work. However, in this story the retribution is repayment by the gods for the evil deeds of men. One of the recurrent themes of the work is that, in the end – and that end might take generations – humans do pay for their actions.

nothing in human life was safe   Cyrus seems to have the wisdom of Solon (and Herodotus) on the fragility of human happiness (see 1.5 (p. 7) and 1.32 (pp. 13–14)).

Apollo   the god of prophecy. His most important shrine was at Delphi, on the north side of the Corinthian Gulf. This was, to the Greeks, the centre of the world. At the oracle, the Pythian priestess, inspired by the god, babbled answers which a priest interpreted into hexameters. Delphi was a central part of Greek life; kings and city-states and individuals consulted Delphi on matters great and small. Just as Delphi was central to the Greek world, so it is a significant element in Herodotus' narrative, not least because the attitude of Delphi to the Persian invasion was not always clear or consistent. In particular, see the ambiguity of the oracle's response to the Athenians' questions in 480 BC (7.140–4).

any of my gifts   after Croesus had decided that Delphi was the most reliable of all oracles, he gave massively impressive gifts which were still visible in Herodotus' time (1.50–1).

'Your majesty,' replied Croesus, '**it was my doing**, and it brought you success and me disaster. But it was **the god of the Greeks who is responsible for this**. He stirred me up to undertake this invasion. For there is no one who is so stupid that he 45 prefers war to peace. For in peace sons bury their fathers. In war fathers bury their sons. I suppose that, somehow or other, **a god wanted this to happen**.'

1.88   This was Croesus' answer to the question and Cyrus set him free from his chains, sat him down next to him and showed him great consideration. Cyrus himself and all those around him **gazed upon him in wonder**, but he remained silent, wrapped 50 in thought.

Then, turning round, Croesus saw that the Persians were plundering the city of the Lydians. 'Your majesty,' he said, '**should I tell you my thoughts** or would it be better for me to be quiet at such a moment?' Cyrus told him to have no fear and say whatever he wanted. So Croesus asked him a question. 'These great crowds 55 of people, what are they doing with such enthusiasm?' And Cyrus said, 'They are plundering your city and carrying off your wealth.' And Croesus replied, 'It is not my city or my wealth that they are plundering. It is not mine any more. It is yours.'

1.89   Cyrus was struck by Croesus' words, so he dismissed everyone else and he asked him his thoughts on what was happening. Croesus said, 'Since the gods have made 60 me your slave, I think it right that I should tell you any of my thoughts. The Persians are, **by nature, a brutal people and they live without possessions**. If you allow them the freedom to plunder and have many possessions, the following is likely to happen: you should expect the man who gets the most to rise up against you. So, if my words please you, do as I say. At every gate, station your bodyguards. They 65

---

it was my doing, the god of the Greeks who is responsible for this, a god wanted this to happen   Croesus' account of responsibility is, at this stage, muddled, in that he accepts that he did it, but doesn't take responsibility. Responsibility is more complex than he understands. Not only is there human responsibility and the gods' will, but the workings of fate.

gazed upon him in wonder   in the same way, and using the same words, Achilles, the greatest of the Greek heroes, and Priam, the king of Troy, who has come to ransom Hector, his dead son, gaze in wonder upon each other at the end of the *Iliad* (24.629–33).

should I tell you my thoughts   throughout Herodotus' narrative there is the problem of the subject telling the truth (or not) to his master. Artabanus (7.10, pp. 55–8), Demaratus (7.101, p. 75) and Artemisia (8.68, pp. 104–5) tell the truth to Xerxes, as Croesus does to Cyrus, but it can be a risky business.

by nature, a brutal people and they live without possessions   Croesus here brings into the narrative one of the key themes, the nature of place and the impact it has on the people who live there. That is why much of Herodotus' history is concerned with people and places. Croesus foresees one danger of excessive prosperity. This warning must be compared with the final story of the whole work, Cyrus' rejection of Artembares' advice that the Persians should leave their homeland (9.122, p. 146).

should take everything from those who are carrying things out of the city and say that it is necessary that a tenth should be dedicated to Zeus. If you do that, they won't be angry with you for taking it from them by force. They will acknowledge that you are doing the right thing and hand things over willingly.'

1.90   When he heard this, Cyrus was absolutely delighted at such good advice. He 70 thanked Croesus and told his bodyguard to do what Croesus had advised. He said to him: 'Croesus, although you are a king, you are ready to do me good in word and deed. Ask for some reward. Whatever you want will be yours immediately.' And he said, 'Master, you will please me most if you allow me to send these fetters and ask the god of the Greeks, whom I honoured most of all, whether it is normal 75 for him to deceive those who do good to him.'

Cyrus then asked what he meant by such a request and Croesus told him all about the oracle's replies and most of all about the offerings he made and how he had been led on by the oracle to invade Persia. He ended his words by asking again for permission to make this criticism of the god.   80

Cyrus **laughed** and said, 'Croesus, I will do this for you and anything else you ask in future.' When Croesus heard this, he sent some Lydians to Delphi and told them to place the fetters on the threshold of the temple and to ask the god whether he wasn't at all ashamed that his oracles had stirred Croesus into the invasion of Persia to destroy Cyrus' power. They were to show him the fetters and say that 85 these were the spoils from that war. This is what they were to ask and whether it was normal for Greek gods to be so ungrateful.

1.91   When the Lydians arrived and said what they had been told to say, the **Pythia** is said to have made the following reply. '**It is impossible, even for a god, to avoid that which has been fated.** Croesus has paid for **a crime committed four** 90 **generations ago.** His ancestor, a bodyguard of the Heracleidae, was lured into a

---

laughed   Cyrus, like Xerxes (7.103, p. 75), laughs and accepts advice, but laughter is not always the right response to advice nor is it always the only response in Herodotus' narrative.

Pythia   the priestess (see note on Apollo at 1.87) who is inspired by the god to speak the prophecy which the priests then interpret.

It is impossible, even for a god, to avoid that which has been fated   the Greeks thought that the gods were powerful, but not all powerful. There was beyond them the overarching power of fate, embodied in the three Fates. In Homer not even Zeus can change fate, although he does toy with the notion (e.g. *Iliad* 16.435–8). However, not every detail is fixed by fate, so there are spaces where the gods can enact their personal desire.

a crime committed four generations ago   Croesus' family came to power when Candaules, the king of Sardis, was murdered by his wife and Gyges, a member of the palace guard. Croesus was a descendant of Gyges. This is the first major story that Herodotus tells after the recounting of the mythical tales of heroine-stealing (1.6–14). This concept of divine punishment across the generations is also found in the Old Testament: it is one way of explaining inexplicable suffering.

woman's plot and killed his master. Thereby he held his master's position that was not rightfully his. **Loxias** had wanted the fall of Sardis to take place in the time of Croesus' children and not in the time of Croesus himself, but he could not deflect the Fates. However, they had made some concession and he had done all he could to help him. He had delayed the capture of Sardis by three years, and Croesus really ought to know that it had been captured that much later than was fated. And, secondly, he had come to his aid when he was on the burning pyre. So Croesus was wrong to blame the oracle for what had happened. What Loxias had actually said was that, **if he invaded Persia, he would destroy a great empire**. If he were going to make a good decision, he should have sent a second time after that and asked whether the oracle meant his own kingdom or that of Cyrus. Since he didn't understand what he was told and didn't even ask, he should really hold himself responsible. As for the final question, Loxias explained about **the mule**. He hadn't even understood that. For Cyrus was the mule: he was not born of two people of the same race, but his mother was of nobler stock than his father. She was **a Mede and the daughter of Astyages, the king of Persia**, but the father was a Persian and a subject and, being of lower birth than all of them, he married his own mistress.'

This was the Pythia's reply to the Lydians. They carried it back to Sardis and told Croesus. When he heard the reply, he realised that the fault was his, and not the god's.

Loxias   a cult title for Apollo.

if he invaded Persia, he would destroy a great empire, the mule   these were the oracles given to Croesus in 1.53 and 1.55. In the first one, Croesus was told that, if he attacked Cyrus, he would destroy a great kingdom. In the second oracle, he was told that he would rule until a mule ruled Persia. This happened in that Cyrus was a mule, the child of a mother nobler than his father, as a mule has a horse for a mother and a donkey for a father. They are typical Delphic utterances, the one apparently clear, but fulfilled unexpectedly, the latter enigmatic. Croesus' faults were not to ask for clarification and not to think harder. In 480 BC the Athenians received a very depressing oracle from Delphi, but asked for a second opinion and then Themistocles used his intelligence to get to the right answer (see 7.140–4). It is worth comparing the prophecies given to Shakespeare's Macbeth in Act 4 Scene 1.

a Mede and the daughter of Astyages, the king of Persia   Cyrus' mother was Mandane, the daughter of Astyages, who was the king of Persia. Influenced by a dream, Astyages chose to marry his daughter not to a Mede of equal rank, but to Cambyses, a Persian who was inferior (1.107–8). Later, Astyages tried to put the child Cyrus to death and the story of his survival, with similarities to the childhoods of Moses and Oedipus, is told in 1.108–17.

Bacchylides and the vase painting

The illustration on p. 16 of Croesus on his pyre clearly depicts a very different version of the story from that of Herodotus. Croesus does not appear to be a victim of the pyre, but seems to be engaged in an act of self-sacrifice. Another version of the story is also preserved, written by Bacchylides. Bacchylides was a poet who wrote odes to celebrate victories in the great athletic contests of the age, at Olympia, Delphi, Corinth and Nemea. None of Bacchylides' work survives intact, but this fragment on the fate of Croesus, written in 468 BC to celebrate a victory at the Pythian Games, has been preserved.

For Croesus, lord of horse-taming Lydia, was saved once by Apollo of the golden sword when, in fulfilment of the doom decreed by Zeus, Sardis was being sacked by the Persian army.

When he had come to that unlooked-for day, Croesus was not minded to wait for the further woe of grievous slavery. He caused a pyre to be built in front of his courtyard with walls of bronze: he mounted it with his true wife and daughters with fair hair, who wailed inconsolably. Lifting up his hands to high heaven, he cried aloud, 'Where is the gratitude of the gods? Where is Apollo, the son of Leto? The house of Croesus is falling; the Persians are attacking the city; women are led captive from the well-built halls. What once was hateful is now welcome. It is sweetest to die.'

So he spoke and he ordered the attendant to kindle the wooden pyre. The maidens shrieked and threw up their hands to their mother. But when the bright strength of the dread fire began to spread, Zeus brought a dark rain-cloud above it and began to quench the yellow flame.

Nothing is past belief which is brought about by the care of the gods. Apollo carried the old man to the **Hyperboreans** *with his daughters of slender ankle and there gave him rest in return for his piety. For,* **of all mortals, he sent the largest gifts to Delphi.**

Hyperboreans   the Greeks had no fixed notion about life after death: if anything, they thought that it was a gloomy, joyless half-life. However, there are various stories told about rewards given to the good. One of them involves the Elysian Fields; another sends them off to the land of the Hyperboreans, the land beyond the north wind.

of all mortals, he sent the largest gifts to Delphi   this, and other details, tally with Herodotus' account (see 1.50–1). Any narrative that had its source in Delphi would be likely to emphasize the value of generosity to Apollo as a way of increasing the chance of future prosperity.

1 These events occurred at least a century before Herodotus was writing. What different sources does he refer to? What others would there have been? How reliable would they have been?

2 How does Herodotus tell his story? What are the strengths of such a method? How does it differ from a modern historical method?

3 How do Solon and Croesus differ in character and values?

4 What are the key themes which Herodotus introduces into his narrative? In what way do they prepare us for the narrative ahead?

5 What does the story tell us about the attitude of the Greeks, Croesus and Cyrus to the gods?

6 'Man is all chance.' Does the life of Croesus suggest that Solon is right?

7 Why does Herodotus give his first major narrative to the story of Croesus?

8 It is almost impossible that Solon and Croesus could have met. In that case, how does such a story come into common currency? If they didn't meet, what, if anything, is the value of Herodotus' story?

9 What do the differing versions of the narrative in Bacchylides or in the vase painting tell us about the world of stories in which Herodotus operated?

3 Egypt and the wonders of the world

In his first sentences Herodotus says that his work will be about 'great and wondrous deeds, some performed by the Greeks, some by non-Greeks'. 'Great and wondrous deeds' has a very broad meaning in that Herodotus is deeply interested in the diversity of human experience and of the world in which he lives. He writes, therefore, about what we now call geography, anthropology, history and religion – indeed about anything that is unusual – and the narrative of the Persian Wars does not begin until he is two-thirds of the way through his work. The narrative is structured around the expansion of the Persian empire, so that he describes each country – Egypt, India, Scythia, Libya – as it comes under Persian control. However, this diverse narrative is not just for the wonder of it all. It helps us to understand ourselves and the world. Herodotus believes that there is a very strong link between a country and the nature of its people, and in the end that is part of the explanation of the Greeks' victory over the Persians. Herodotus also wants to show us something that is timeless, that the customs of people differ, but that doesn't mean that one is superior to the other.

Herodotus gives most attention to Egypt. He tells us that he travelled extensively there and that the country had a great fascination. It had a civilization much older and more spectacular than that of the Greeks and the topography was very different. Indeed, as 2.35 (pp. 27–8) shows, Herodotus conceived of Egypt as the mirror-image of Greek culture. Herodotus doesn't get everything right about Egypt, but on some matters, like mummification, his is the only written record that survives.

The closest parallel to much of Herodotus' writing on this subject is *The Travels of Marco Polo*. Marco Polo set out from Venice in 1271 and travelled to the court of Kublai Khan in China.

The Nile and the reason for it flooding: 2.19–26

Most Greek rivers are short and steep, briefly torrents in the winter, but dried up in the summer. The Nile, therefore, was a wonder, not only vast, but also flooding extensively in the summer. Herodotus' attempt to account for this is misguided, both in choosing the wrong explanation and in rejecting the right one, but he does apply observation, logic and the ideas of others in a coherent and structured way.

2.19 When **the Nile** floods, it spreads over not only the Delta but in some places over land which is said to be part of Libya and Arabia to an extent of **two days' journey** on either side. Sometimes it is more and sometimes less than this. As for the nature of the river, I could gain **no information from either the priests or anyone else.** I was especially eager to find out why the Nile **floods from the time of the summer solstice for 100 days,** and, when it comes close to this number of days, it retreats and reduces its stream. Then it continues to be low during the whole winter until the summer solstice comes round again. I couldn't find out anything from any Egyptian on these matters, although I asked them what it was about the Nile that meant it was the opposite of other rivers. I kept on making enquiries in my desire to know about this and why it was the only river from which no breezes blow.

2.20 **Some Greeks who are keen to gain a reputation for cleverness** have given three accounts of the river. Of the three of them, I wouldn't think that two of them were worth mentioning if I didn't just want to say what they were. The first explanation says that **etesian winds** are the cause of the flooding of the river since they prevent

the Nile   it is no surprise that the Nile confounds Herodotus. It is over 4,000 miles long and has two major tributaries, the Blue Nile, which rises in Ethiopia, and the White Nile, which rises in Rwanda.

two days' journey   this isn't true along the length of the Nile, but it would have been true for the areas that Herodotus saw.

no information from either the priests or anyone else   Herodotus will have depended on his own eye-witness experience in writing his account, but he must also have spoken to the Egyptians, presumably through interpreters. This reference to the lack of information from the Egyptians may reflect the distinction between Greeks and Egyptians: the former ask questions, particularly the inquisitive Herodotus, whereas the latter don't.

floods from the time of the summer solstice for 100 days   the Nile rises at different times in different places, but the summer solstice isn't far wrong for the flood at Cairo and 100 days is quite accurate, too.

Some Greeks who are keen to gain a reputation for cleverness   Herodotus may get nothing from the Egyptians, but he is also quick to criticize his fellow Greeks. Thales of Miletus, whom Herodotus refers to in 1.74 and 1.170, attributes the flood to the effect of the etesian winds. Hecataeus of Miletus and others said that the Nile flowed from Ocean, and Anaxagoras of Clazomenae attributed the flood to melting snows. Thales and Anaxagoras were major figures in early natural philosophy (see *Early Greek Philosophy*, edited by Jonathan Barnes – see Recommended reading) and Hecataeus was the most important of Herodotus' predecessors in the recording of the past.

etesian winds   these winds blow from the north-west during the summer and so, according to the theory, would have driven the waters of the Nile back at that time of year.

the Nile from flowing out into the sea. However, there are lots of times when the etesian winds don't blow and the Nile still does the same thing. Furthermore, **if the etesian winds were the reason**, then the same thing would have to happen to the other rivers which flow against the direction of the etesian winds as happens to the Nile. Indeed, it would have to happen to them all the more to the extent that 20 they are smaller and have a weaker water flow. There are many rivers in Syria and Libya which do not behave like the Nile.

2.21   The second explanation is more senseless than the one I've just mentioned, but it is the more remarkable. This says that the Nile does this because it flows from **Ocean** and Ocean flows all the way round the earth.   25

2.22   The third explanation is by far the most plausible but it is the **most mistaken**. For this explanation offers nothing of worth. It says that the Nile flows from melting snow, this very river that flows out of Libya and the middle of Ethiopia and discharges into Egypt. How on earth could its source be snow, flowing, as it does, from the hottest places to places that are predominantly cooler? Anyone 30 capable of the slightest capacity for reason could see that it is not likely that its source could be the snow. The strongest piece of evidence is that the winds that blow from these regions are hot. The second is that the land is without rainfall and there is never a frost. It is inevitable that there is rain within five days of a snowfall. So it must be that if there were snow in these areas, there would also 35 be rain. The third piece of evidence is that the people there are black from the heat. And kites and swallows don't migrate from there in the course of the year, and cranes, to escape the winter in Scythia, go to pass the winter in these areas. Therefore, if it snowed to the slightest degree in the areas through which the Nile flowed or where it rises, none of this would be the case. Necessity proves it.   40

---

if the etesian winds were the reason   Herodotus may come to the wrong conclusion, but he does employ logical methods and brings to bear other empirical evidence in an intelligent way. It is worth noting the recurrent use of words for evidence and logical argument. (See Rosalind Thomas, *Herodotus in Context*, pp. 182–5, for an account of his argument. She argues that Herodotus has learnt something of this method from the writings of Hippocrates, who employs the same methods on disease.)

Ocean   the Greeks thought that the land mass was surrounded by the stream of Ocean: in *Iliad* 18.607–8 Ocean encircles the world on the shield of Achilles. According to this theory, the Nile would be unique as a river because it did not rise somewhere in the mountains but flowed directly from the waters that surrounded the world.

most mistaken   Herodotus is unfortunate that he rejects so readily the right answer: the Nile is fed by the heavy rains that fall on the Abyssinian plain. He was not to know that the world did not just keep on getting hotter and drier.

2.23   The man who talked about Ocean has taken his account into the **obscurity of myth** which does not allow of any proof. I don't know of any river called Ocean, but I imagine that **Homer** or some other poet from the past found the name and introduced it into his work.

2.24   But if, having found fault with the theories proposed by others, I must express 45 my own theory about these matters of uncertainty, I'll tell you what seems to me to be the reason for the Nile's flooding in the summer. During the winter season **the sun is driven by storms out of its original path to the upper areas of Libya.** So that's my complete account, to express it in the shortest possible form. For it is reasonable that the land to which **this god** is closest should be most affected by a 50 shortage of water and the flow of the rivers of that area should be diminished.

2.25   A fuller account is as follows. As the sun passes over the upper regions of Libya it acts as follows. In these regions the air is clear at all times and the land is hot and has no cooling winds. So the sun, as it passes over there, does what it does here when it is at its height. **It attracts water towards itself** and, having done so, it then 55 pushes it inland where the winds take it up and scatter it so that it is dispersed. It is reasonable, therefore, that the winds that blow from this region, the south and the south-west winds, should be by far the wettest of all winds. I think it likely that the sun doesn't get rid of all the annual water from the Nile each time, but rather keeps back some of it around itself. When the winter is softening, the sun returns 60 to its former course in the middle of the heavens and from then on it attracts water from all rivers equally. During this time all the rivers that are fed by a great amount of rainwater and flow through terrain with rain and deep channels flow with great force. But during the summer, when rainfall is lacking and they are

---

obscurity of myth   Herodotus rejects myth as an acceptable source of evidence. Compare his use of myth, rationalized by the Persians, in the story of the kidnaps of 1.1–5 (pp. 3–7).

Homer   the author of the *Iliad* and the *Odyssey*, the two great epic poems composed at the end of the eighth century BC that mark the beginning of Greek literature. The stories of Homer's origins are manifold, but nothing is known for sure, although he, like Herodotus, was a product of Ionia. As the old line goes, 'The *Iliad* wasn't written by Homer, but by another man of the same name.'

the sun is driven by storms out of its original path to the upper areas of Libya   this picture is dependent on the idea that the earth is a disc covered by the dome of the heavens. In such an enclosed universe, the sun can get blown off course by the winds, just as the clouds are blown about the sky.

this god   Herodotus refers to Apollo, the god of the sun, just as Artemis is the goddess of the moon.

It attracts water towards itself   Herodotus' account may be wrong, but it is ingenious. It is based upon the key observation that the sun draws moisture upwards from the earth. So he shows that people are wrong to think that the Nile's behaviour is odd in summer, when it floods. In fact, the odd thing about its behaviour takes place in winter, when it dries up, unlike all other rivers he knows.

being sucked up by the sun, they are weak. Since the Nile is the only river that 65
has no rainfall and is being sucked up by the sun in winter, it is reasonable that it
should be the only river that flows with much less force than in the summer. In
the summer, it is being sucked up at the same rate as all the other rivers. In the
winter it is the only one that suffers in this way. So I have come to the conclusion
that the sun is the reason for this. 70

2.26   And this is also the reason – in my opinion – for the dryness of the air in this
region, since it burns its course through the region. So **in the upper lands of
Libya it is always summer**. If the seasons and the heavens were reversed and the
place occupied by the north wind and the winter were occupied by the south
wind and the heat of noon – if this were to happen, the sun would be driven off 75
course from the middle of heaven by the storms and the north wind and it would
go to the upper regions of Europe as it does now to the upper regions of Libya.
And, as the sun passed over all of Europe, I expect that the **Danube** would do
what the Nile now does. As for the breeze that does not blow, I have this idea that
it is not unreasonable that no breeze should come from very hot places. Rather, it 80
is normally the case that breeze comes from something **cold**.

The wonders of Egypt: 2.35

2.35   I am going to talk at length about Egypt, because it has the most **wonders** of
anywhere in the world and across the whole country it produces monuments
beyond words. For these reasons I will say much about this country. It has
a climate that is different from anywhere else. It has a river that is different in
its nature from other rivers and, in the same way, the customs and laws are all 5
the opposite of those of other people. **Women go out into the town square and
trade, whilst men stay at home and weave.** Everyone else in the world weaves by

---

in the upper lands of Libya it is always summer   Herodotus is very close to right in that
the equatorial regions do have, compared with the Mediterranean, an endless summer.

Danube   the Danube is the other great river known to the Greeks and Herodotus gives
a great deal of coverage to this river, too (see 4.47–51). Herodotus believes that there is
symmetry in the geography of the world and that the Danube is, in effect, the Nile of
the north.

cold   Herodotus doesn't understand that winds come from a difference in pressure.
However, he is trying to think logically with what he does know.

wonders   this word takes us back to the first sentence of Herodotus' work. Herodotus'
picture of Egypt as the world in a mirror is overschematic: there is evidence of each of
the things he mentions, but it is not the case that all Egyptians did all the things that he
describes. However, he is trying to make sense of the world.

**Women go out into the town square and trade, whilst men stay at home and
weave**   Herodotus implicitly tells us what Greek life was like in that women of citizen
families in Greece generally lived secluded lives, not venturing out to the market.

pushing the weft upwards, but Egyptians push it downwards. Men carry burdens on their heads, whilst women carry them on their backs. Women urinate standing up, men do it sitting down. They relieve themselves indoors and eat outdoors in the street. Their argument is that you should do shameful things in private and non-shameful things in public. There are no women priests for male or female gods, and there are male priests for all male and female gods. **It is not compulsory for sons to look after their parents** if they don't want to, whereas it is compulsory for daughters whether they want to or not. 10

15

Cats and crocodiles: 2.66–70

2.66   There are many domesticated animals, but there would be many more if it weren't

for what happens to **cats**. When the female cats give birth, they stop mating with the males and the males who want to mate don't get what they want. So they adopt this clever plan. They steal the young from the females, take them away and then kill them, although they don't eat them. The females, who have lost their young and want more, come back to the males, because they are creatures that love their young. 5

When there is a fire, cats behave in the following extraordinary way. The Egyptians spread out and place guards on the cats, but make no attempt to put out the fire. The cats sneak past or leap over the men and throw themselves into the fires. This causes terrible grief amongst the Egyptians. If a cat dies of natural causes in a house, all the inhabitants shave off their eyebrows. If a dog does the same, they shave their whole bodies and their heads. 10

15

Cats were important in ancient Egypt, both as domestic pets and as deities. The earliest remains of a cat in a tomb suggest that the Egyptians were keeping them as pets as early as the late fourth millennium BC. From about 800 BC onwards, large numbers of sacred cats were mummified, including this one, which was found in Abydos and dates from the Roman period.

It is not compulsory for sons to look after their parents   for Greeks the responsibility for caring for the family rested with the males.

cats   cats were not common in Greece, so for Herodotus they are a novelty. The care that the Egyptians give to animals in life and death is also a novelty to a Greek. Herodotus is wrong about cats, but he is basing his account on three things that are factual: the noise that females make in having sex would make you think that they didn't enjoy it; male cats do, on occasions, kill their young; cats do go back into burning buildings to try to save their young.

2.67   Dead cats are taken to sacred chambers in the city of Boubastos where they are **mummified** and buried. Everyone buries their dogs in their own town in sacred tombs. Mongooses are buried in just the same way as dogs. They take shrews and hawks to the city of Bouto, and ibises to Hermopolis. Bears – which are rare – and wolves – which are not much bigger than foxes – are buried wherever they are 20 found.

2.68   **Crocodiles** are like this. **For the four coldest months of the year, the crocodile eats nothing.** It has four legs and lives on land and in the water. It produces and hatches its eggs on land and spends most of the day there, but it spends all night in the river because the water is warmer than the air and the moisture. Of all the 25 creatures we know, the crocodile has the biggest difference in size between birth and maturity. It produces eggs that are no bigger than a goose's, and the new-born creature matches it in size, but it can grow to a size of **17 cubits**, or even more. It has the eyes of a pig, big, projecting fangs, and it is **the only animal that doesn't have a tongue. It doesn't move its bottom jaw**; it is the only animal that moves its 30 top jaw towards its bottom jaw. It has strong claws and a thick, scaly, impenetrable skin. It is **blind in the water**, but on land it has the most acute eyesight. Since it lives in the water, its mouth is full of **leeches**. All other birds and animals stay out of its way except the **sandpiper**. This bird lives at peace with the crocodile because it does it a service. When the crocodile comes out of the water onto dry land and 35 then yawns – it usually does this facing westwards – the sandpiper nips down into its mouth and eats the leeches. The crocodile is glad of this help, so it does the sandpiper no harm.

---

mummified   the mummies of many animals, domestic and wild, have been preserved. This care for animals is clearly related to the animal forms that the gods take in Egyptian religion.

Crocodiles   to some extent Hecataeus (see note on 2.20) is thought to be the source for this account. However, it has its own charm: in its apparently random collocation of 'facts' – many of which are untrue – it does sound like someone trying to describe to a friend something 'wondrous'. On the other hand, Aristotle (*History of Animals* 5.33) does make extensive use of Herodotus in his description. It is worth comparing Marco Polo's account of a giraffe, which isn't much better (see Marco Polo, *The Travels*, p. 302).

For the four coldest months of the year, the crocodile eats nothing   this isn't true, but the crocodile is less seen in the winter and can live for long periods without food.

17 cubits   over 20 feet, but that isn't too much of an exaggeration: the Nile crocodile can reach 15 feet.

the only animal that doesn't have a tongue. It doesn't move its bottom jaw   both of these statements are incorrect. The crocodile only has a very small tongue, but it does have one, and it looks as though it doesn't move its bottom jaw, but it does.

blind in the water   not true; the crocodile has very good eyesight in the water.

leeches   there are no leeches in the Nile.

sandpiper   the sandpiper does eat small creatures out of the mouth of the crocodile.

2.69   Crocodiles are sacred to some of the Egyptians, but not others and these people treat them as enemies. They are especially sacred to the people who live around 40 Thebes and Lake Moeris. In those areas everyone adopts and looks after one particular crocodile. They teach it to be tame and they put glass and gold pendants on its ears and bracelets round its front feet and they give it special food and the sacrificial victims to eat. They do all they can to give it the best possible life. When the animals die, they mummify and bury them in sacred tombs. However, the 45 people who live around Elephantine don't think they are sacred; they even eat them. They don't call them crocodiles, but *champsai*. It was the Ionians who called them crocodiles, which means lizards, thinking that they were like the lizards that live in stone walls.

2.70   There are many different ways of **hunting the crocodile**, but I am going to write 50 about the way that seems most worth telling. The hunter baits a hook with the chine of a pig and lets it out into the middle of the river. He also has with him on the bank of the river a live pig and he beats it. When the crocodile hears the pig's squealing, it makes for the sound. When it comes upon the pig chine, it gulps it down and that's how they catch it. When they have landed it on the bank, the first 55 thing that the hunter does is smear its eyes with mud. If the hunter does this, then overpowering the crocodile is easy. If he didn't, it would be a real problem.

Mummification: 2.85–89

2.85   This is how they conduct **the mourning and burial of their dead**. When it is a man of some repute who is departing from his house, all the women of that household smear their heads and faces with mud. Then they leave the corpse in the house and they wander the streets accompanied by all their relations, with their clothing undone and exposing their breasts. The men also do the same thing 5 elsewhere, with their clothing undone and beating their breasts. When they have done this, they take the corpse for **mummification**.

---

hunting the crocodile   compare Marco Polo's account of catching whales (see Marco Polo, *The Travels*, pp. 296–7).

the mourning and burial of their dead   as Herodotus' story of Darius, the Indians and the Greeks shows (see 3.38, p. 33), the difference in burial systems is a striking feature of different cultures. Indeed, Herodotus' interest in the subject is a precursor of the way anthropologists use changes in burial customs to chart the changes of cultures.

mummification   the Greeks burnt their dead (see 3.38 (p. 33) and Patroclus' funeral in Homer's *Iliad* 23.192–218), so the Egyptian approach to the dead was particularly remarkable. The Egyptians believed the survival of the body was essential for the survival of the spirit, but the Greeks had no such concept. Herodotus' account of mummification is also remarkable: for all the survival of mummies, his is the only written account of the process that survives and recent research has largely supported his account.

2.86   There are people who are engaged in this business and have this expertise. When a corpse is brought to them, they show those who have brought it samples of wooden corpses, painted to be life-like. They say that 10 the finest form of embalming is **sacred to the god** whose name it would be sacrilegious for me to name in this context. They also show the second type, which is inferior and cheaper, and the third type, which is the cheapest. They describe all this and they then ask them how they want the corpse to be prepared. When 15 they have agreed a price, the relatives depart. The embalmers are left in the house and this is how they perform the finest form of mummification. First of all, **they remove the brain through the nostrils with an iron spoon.** They get some of it out by this method and they get the rest out by means of drugs. Then they 20 make an incision along the flank with a sharp Ethiopian stone knife and they remove the internal organs through this incision. The next thing they do is purify and clean out the body cavity with palm wine and then again with crushed spices. Then, they fill the belly with pure, crushed myrrh and cassia and other spices 25 – but not frankincense – and stitch it up again. After they have done this, they **preserve the body in natrum** and keep it there for 70 days. They shouldn't do it for any longer than this. When the 70 days have been completed, they wash the corpse and wrap the whole body in linen bandages cut into strips. The bandages are 30 impregnated with gum which the Egyptians usually use instead of glue. At this point the relatives collect the body and they make a wooden casket in human form and they enclose the body in a case and lock it. Finally, they store the casket in a burial chamber, standing it up against the wall.   35

This is the sarcophagus containing the mummy of the priest Nesperennub and dates to around 800 BC. It was discovered in the 1890s in Luxor.

sacred to the god   the god whom Herodotus does not mention is Osiris. He rules the world of the dead and the mummy is made to look like Osiris so that the dead person could gain access to Osiris' world.

they remove the brain through the nostrils with an iron spoon   surviving mummies have no brains in the cranial cavity and they also have a hole drilled through from the nostrils into the brain.

preserve the body in natrum   natrum removes the water from the corpse. For a long time Herodotus' account was questioned, but that was because the Greek word he uses for 'preserve' was translated as 'immerse in'.

2.87 This is the most expensive way of preparing corpses. However, for those who want the mid-priced version, avoiding great expense, they do as follows. They fill syringes with cedar oil and they inject this into the body cavity. They don't make an incision or remove the organs, but they inject it up the back passage and put a bung in to stop it flowing out. They embalm it for the prescribed number of days, and on the 40 final day they draw off from the cavity the cedar oil which they had injected earlier. This has the effect of removing the belly and guts which have been dissolved in the oil. The natrum eats the flesh so that all that is left of the corpse is the skin and bones. When they have done this they give it back and do nothing more.

2.88 The third method, which is the one adopted by those who are short of money, is as 45 follows. They clean out the body cavity with myrrh and embalm it for seventy days. Then they give it to the relatives to take it away.

2.89 When the wife of a great man dies, or any woman who was particularly beautiful or of high repute, they don't give her over to be mummified at once. Instead they do so after three or four days have gone by. **The reason for this is so that the mummifiers** 50 **should not have sex** with the women. They say that one of them was caught having sex with the fresh corpse of a woman and he was denounced by a fellow-worker.

Darius and the treatment of the dead: 3.38

> In Book 3 Herodotus recounts Cambyses' conquest of Egypt and his subsequent descent into madness. He killed his own brother and sister and showed no respect for Egyptian religious customs. This prompts Herodotus to tell one of the most important stories in the book, showing the author's understanding of and respect for cultural differences.

3.38 It is clear to me that **Cambyses** was completely mad. If he had not been, he would not have set about mocking sacred objects and traditions. Suppose someone were to propose to everyone in the world that they should choose the customs that they thought to be the best of all. Everyone, after due consideration, would choose their own. Everyone thinks that their own customs are by far the best. It is not likely that 5 anyone other than a madman would laugh at such things.

The reason for this is so that the mummifiers should not have sex   there is a kind of comfort that even Herodotus can succumb to sensationalism and a ghoulish fascination with necrophilia.

Cambyses   the eldest son of Cyrus, he became king of Persia on his father's death in 530 BC. His greatest achievement was the conquest of Egypt (3.4–13), but Herodotus records growing evidence of Cambyses' madness in his narrative (see 3.16, 30–7). He died in 522 BC as he was returning to Persia from Egypt on the news that his brother, Smerdis, had usurped the throne (3.61–6).

It is possible to conclude that all mankind think the same thing about their customs from many other pieces of evidence, but particularly from this story. Some Greeks happened to be with Darius in his kingdom and Darius called them to him and asked how much money they would want to eat their dead fathers. They said that 10 they wouldn't do that for any money. After this Darius summoned some Indians called the **Callatiae** who eat their parents and he asked them, in the presence of the Greeks – who could understand what was said through an interpreter – how much money they would accept to burn their dead fathers on a pyre. They shouted out loud and told him not to say such dreadful things. So that is how customs are, and 15 **Pindar** is right when he says that **custom** is 'king of all'.

India, Arabia and the far north: 3.101–6, 111, 113–16

In these chapters Herodotus is describing things that he has certainly never seen, and, of course, travellers' tales have the habit of growing in the telling. Some of the things that he gets wrong are prejudices that have survived for hundreds, if not thousands, of years. However, he does get some things right and at least the range of his interest does bring Britain, the Tin Islands, into the world of Greek history.

Callatiae   Herodotus doesn't mention this Indian tribe elsewhere, although in 4.26 he does refer to another tribe that eats its dead.

Pindar   the most famous lyric poet of the early fifth century BC and a contemporary of Bacchylides (see p. 21). The most important, and best preserved, part of his work is *The Odes*, composed for victorious competitors in the great athletic festivals of Greece. These are preserved as the Olympian odes (for victors at Olympia), the Pythian odes (for victors at Delphi), the Isthmian ode (for victors at the Isthmian Games at Corinth) and the Nemean odes (for victors at Nemea). From such apparently unpromising beginnings, Pindar created immensely complex poetry, rich in myth and moral guidance. His other works survive in fragments, of which this quotation (Fragment 152) is one.

custom   the Greek word is *nomos*, which can be translated as 'custom' or 'law'. When Demaratus speaks in 7.104 (p. 78) of the Spartans' way as 'freedom under the law', he uses the word *nomos*. Here Herodotus makes his contribution to one of the key issues of debate in the fifth century BC: the relationship between nature (*phusis*, as in the English word 'physics') and law or custom. To what extent is human action formed by that which is natural or how much of it is conditioned by the culture in which one grows up? Are there certain immutable laws of human behaviour that are common to all? The most significant representation of the possible conflict is Sophocles' *Antigone*. The king Creon had decreed that Polynices should be left unburied for fighting against his city. Polynices' sister, Antigone, believes that the burial of her brother is an eternal law that no king's decree can override.

king of all   an extended version of this quotation is also preserved in Plato's dialogue *Gorgias* (484b): 'Custom is king of all, men and gods alike. It carries things off with a high hand, making might to be right.'

3.101 All the Indians I have described **have sexual intercourse in public, like animals**. They are all the same colour and almost as black as the Ethiopians. The semen that they ejaculate into their wives isn't white like the semen of other people, but is as black as their skins. The semen of Ethiopians is black, too. These Indians live a long way from the Persians to the south and they were not under the rule of King Darius. 5

3.102 There are other Indians whose land borders on the city of **Caspaturos** and the land of **Pactya**. They live to the north of the other Indians. Their way of life resembles that of the **Bactrians** and they are the most warlike of the Indians. They are also the Indians who send expeditions for **gold**. The sand renders this part of 10 the country uninhabitable. In this deserted, sandy territory there are **ants** that are smaller than dogs but bigger than foxes. At the Persian king's court there are some that have been taken into captivity. These ants make their homes by digging into the sand in the same way as ants in Greece and they are very similar in appearance. The sand that they throw up contains gold. The Indians send expeditions to get 15 this gold. They each yoke up three camels, with male camels on either side like trace horses and the female in the middle. The Indian rides the middle camel. He ensures that he yokes a female that has been snatched away from its newly born young. These female camels are just as fast as horses, but, in addition to this, they are capable of carrying much heavier burdens. 20

3.103 I'm not going to describe the appearance of a camel because Greeks already know. However, I am going to say something that isn't known. A camel has four thighs and **four knees** in its two hind legs, and its **genitals** face backwards, towards the tail.

---

have sexual intercourse in public, like animals compare 1.203 for another tribe who reach this lowest form of human life.

Caspaturos the editors of the *Cambridge Ancient History* think that Caspaturos is Peshawar, but not everyone is so sure.

Pactya Pactya means 'mountain border-land'. It is the place from which Scylax started his remarkable voyage (4.44).

Bactrians Bactria is north of Afghanistan and the Hindu Kush.

gold, ants Herodotus' account puts together a number of things that are true: gold is abundant in this area; ant heaps do contain gold dust; the Persian word for marmot was 'mountain ant'. However, the account of the difficulty and danger of gold-gathering may just be a means of keeping rivals from entering the market. Compare Marco Polo's account of fishing for pearls (see Marco Polo, *The Travels*, pp. 260–2).

four knees the camel does not have four knees, or four thighs in its hind legs. However, the camel does seem to have more than one joint in its leg as it kneels down because of the length of its metatarsal bone, so that it is an easy mistake to make.

genitals a camel's genitals do face backwards.

3.104 This is the method the Indians adopt in yoking the animals. They set out to get 25
the gold, having made careful calculations to ensure that they get there to take the
gold at the hottest time of the day because the ants disappear underground in the
heat. In these parts **the sun is at its hottest in the morning**, between sunrise and
the time when the market place closes down, whereas for everyone else it is hottest
at noon. It is much hotter at this time here than it is at noon in Greece, to such 30
a degree that the Indians are said to drench themselves in water at this time. The
mid-day heat is almost the same here as it is elsewhere, and, as the sun goes down
in the afternoon, it's about as hot here as elsewhere in the morning. After this it
goes cold, so that at sunset it is very cold indeed.

3.105 When the Indians get to the place, they fill the sacks they have brought with sand 35
and then they head off as quickly as they can. According to the Indians, if they
didn't get a head start whilst the ants are gathering, none of them would survive.
Male camels are slower runners than females so, when they can't keep up, they cut
them loose one at a time. But the females, remembering the young that they have
left behind, show no weakness. So this is the way, according to the Persians, that 40
the Indians get most of their gold, although they get small quantities by digging it
out of the ground.

3.106 For some reason, the most remote parts of the inhabited world have the finest
products, although Greece has by far the finest **mixed climate**. For example, India
is the most easterly part of the inhabited world, as I have just said, and there 45
they have animals, both land animals and birds, that are much bigger than in
other countries. The exception is in the case of horses and here Median horses,
called Nesaean, are superior. Secondly, there are endless supplies of gold here,
some of it excavated, some of it carried down by rivers, some of it stolen as I have
just described. Furthermore, here wild trees produce as their fruit a **wool** which is 50
superior in beauty and quality to that which comes from sheep. The Indians make
their clothes from it.

3.111 The Arabians collect cinnamon in a really amazing way. They cannot say where it
comes from or which land produces it, except to the extent that they apply logic and

---

the sun is at its hottest in the morning   this is not true, but it has a logic in Herodotus'
picture of the world: if the earth is a disc under a dome, then the east, where the sun
rises, must be hottest first. In the same way it is likely to be the coldest at the end of the
day.

mixed climate   Herodotus thinks that Ionia has the easiest climate for human beings and
that the hardest climates are at the edges of the world. There is in the world a natural
order so that the extremities produce the extremes of climate and animal and vegetable
life (see 3.108 for Herodotus' account of the balance in nature and 3.116 (p. 37) for his
account of the extremes at the edge of the world).

wool   wool on trees is cotton.

say that it is produced in the lands **where Dionysus was brought up.** They say that 55
great birds carry these sticks which we, following the Phoenicians, call cinnamon,
and they bring them to their nests which are made out of mud on sheer crags and
are inaccessible to men. The Arabians have adopted the following plan to deal with
this. They cut up dead cattle and donkeys and other beasts of burden into the biggest
possible pieces, take them there, leave them near the **nests** and then get out of the 60
way. The birds fly down and carry the pieces of meat up to their nests. However, the
nests can't stand the weight and they come crashing down to the ground. Then the
Arabians come back and collect it. So this is the way that cinnamon is collected and
then it is exported everywhere else.

3.113   That is all I have to say about fragrant spices, but a miraculous sweetness does 65
emanate from the land of Arabia. There are also two amazing types of sheep there
that aren't found anywhere else. One species has a long tail, not less than three
cubits. If the animals had to drag these around, they would get sores from rubbing
their tails on the ground. In fact, every shepherd knows enough about woodwork to
make **little trolleys** and put them under the tails: they tie the tail of every animal to 70
a little trolley. The other species of sheep has a broad tail, about a cubit in width.

3.114   In the south-west, in the direction where the noonday sun slips away towards
sunset, Ethiopia is the most remote of the inhabited lands. The country produces
great quantities of gold, an abundance of elephants, every type of wild tree and
ebony and **the biggest and most beautiful and longest-living men in the world.** 75

3.115   These are the furthest parts of Asia and Libya. As for the furthest parts of western
Europe, I cannot speak with accuracy. I do not accept that there is a river, called
Eridanos by the barbarians, which flows into the northern sea and which is, or

---

where Dionysus was brought up Herodotus presumably means Ethiopia, where
festivals were held in the god's honour (3.97). Dionysus was snatched from the womb of
his mother, Semele, and had to be brought up away from the jealous eyes of Hera. Hence
he had a very migratory early life.

nests   compare the story in Marco Polo, *The Travels* (pp. 272–3), of how diamonds are
obtained.

little trolleys   barbary sheep do have enormous tails, some of them weighing as much
as 70 pounds, and they are still protected at times by wheeled boards. Marco Polo also
refers to such sheep in Persia (see Marco Polo, *The Travels*, p. 64).

the biggest and most beautiful and longest-living men in the world   Herodotus believes
that the products of the edges of the world are the most extraordinary and exotic
(see 3.116, p. 37).

Eridanos   the word originally just means 'river' (compare the Celtic word 'avon') and
it lives on in the names Rhône and Rhine. It is referred to in Hesiod's *Theogony* 338, a
poem from the late eighth century BC. If the name of the river is to be linked with amber,
it is likely that the river is the Rhône, which was a very important route north through
France.

so they say, the source of amber. Nor am I sure that the **Tin Islands** exist, from which we get tin. In the first instance, the name of Eridanos itself argues against its existence: it is a Greek name, not a barbarian one, and it has been **invented by some poet**. In the second, I've made a real effort, but I have not been able to find anyone who has actually seen for himself that there is a river beyond Europe. Nevertheless, we do get tin and amber from the most remote places. [80]

3.116   It is clear that the north of Europe has by far the greatest supply of gold. But as for [85] why that is, I can't even tell you that with any accuracy. One account is that the **one-eyed Arimaspians** steal it from the gryphons. I am not convinced that there are one-eyed men who are like other humans in all other respects. It is likely that the furthest parts of the world, being enclosed and separate from other countries, should have the things that appear to us to be the most beautiful and most rare. [90]

> 1   What are the most striking features of Herodotus' writings about other places?
>
> 2   What sources and methods does Herodotus use to understand and explain what he sees?
>
> 3   What qualities, good and bad, does Herodotus show in these passages?
>
> 4   What other examples are there of writers dealing with the unfamiliar? How do they compare?

Tin Islands   this must be Britain, or at least a part of Britain.

invented by some poet   Herodotus continues his disdain of the poets, whom he accuses of invention and lack of reliability (see his opinion of Homer on Ocean in 2.23, p. 26).

one-eyed Arimaspians   4.13 shows us Herodotus' picture of the wildness and savagery of life in the north.

4 The battle of Marathon, 490 BC

Sardis, the capital of Croesus' kingdom, was captured by the Persians under Cyrus in 546 BC, and the fall of Lydia brought the Persian empire into direct contact with the Greeks of Ionia (see note on Herodotus on p. 2) for the first time. Books 2 to 4 of Herodotus follow the expansion of the Persian empire, but in Book 5 the narrative returns to the Greek world and the Ionian revolt. In 499 BC, the major cities of Ionia revolted against Persia and even sacked Sardis (5.99–103). Before the revolt, the Ionians came to mainland Greece in search of assistance in their revolt, and Athens and two cities on Euboea – Chalcis and Eretria – supplied it. In the end the revolt was subdued in 494 BC, and many cities of Ionia were sacked and started to pay tribute to the Persians.

After the suppression of the revolt the Persian king Darius wanted revenge on the Greek cities that had interfered in his affairs. In 5.105 Herodotus tells us that Darius ordered one of his attendants to remind him three times a day about the Athenians. So he organized a seaborne attack on Euboea and Athens. However, he himself did not take part: it was led by Datis, a Mede, and Artaphernes, Darius' nephew. They were accompanied by Hippias, who had ruled as a tyrant in Athens from 527 BC until his expulsion in 510 BC (see note on 6.102). The Persians' intention would have been to restore Hippias to power and put an end to the democracy that had been set up in 508 BC, soon after his expulsion.

After taking Chalcis and Eretria (see map on p. 79), the Persian forces landed on the plain of Marathon, in the northern corner of Attica. Here the Athenians enjoyed their finest hour. At Marathon they stood almost alone, with some support from their neighbours Plataea, against the barbarians. When the Persians invaded again in 480 BC, they had to share the credit. Marathon encapsulated Athenian self-image, much as the battle of Trafalgar or the battle of Britain did for the British, or the battle of Yorktown for Americans.

Preparations for battle: 6.102–3, 105–7

6.102   After the **conquest of Eretria** the Persians waited for a few days and then **sailed for Attica**. Their intention was to put the Athenians under intense pressure: they thought that they would do to the Athenians what they had done to the people of Eretria. **Marathon** was the best place in Attica for the use of **cavalry** and it was very close to Eretria. It was for these reasons that **Hippias, the son of Pisistratus,** 5 had brought them there.

6.103   When the Athenians heard the news, they too set out for Marathon. They were led by **ten generals,** of whom **Miltiades** was the tenth.

---

conquest of Eretria   the Greeks of this period were of two distinct groups, the Ionians and the Dorians. The Dorians, who included the Spartans, were the dominant group on mainland Greece, whereas the vast majority of the Ionians lived on the coast of what is now Turkey and the eastern islands of the Aegean. The Greeks called the eastern coast of the Aegean Ionia. The only Ionian Greeks left on the west of the Aegean were the Athenians and the people of Chalcis and Eretria, and this explains their support for the Ionian revolt.

sailed for Attica   Herodotus says that there were 600 ships (6.95). The most recent detailed account of the Persian wars suggests a figure of about 25,000 men for the Persian forces. The Greeks weren't very good at precision when counting big numbers: in Plato's *Menexenus*, a century later, a figure of 500,000 is given.

Marathon   an Athenian village on a flat coastal plain in the northern corner of Attica (see map on p. 79).

cavalry   mainland Greece had very little flat, fertile land, which the breeding of horses requires, so the Greeks were not strong in cavalry. The Persians hoped to set their cavalry against the foot-soldier hoplites. The cavalry's almost complete absence from the narrative of Herodotus and others has generated massive, but inconclusive, scholarly literature.

Hippias, the son of Pisistratus   Athens had been ruled by the family of Pisistratus as tyrants from 546 BC to 510 BC. Many Greek cities at this time were ruled in the same way by dynastic families, and this type of tyranny was not necessarily a bad thing. In 510 BC Hippias' brother, Hipparchus, was assassinated and, soon after, Hippias himself was driven into exile. Two years later Cleisthenes introduced the constitutional change that has been seen as the introduction of the first democracy into western civilization: Herodotus' account is in 5.55–66. In 490 there would still have been those amongst the aristocratic families who would have wanted the end of the new democracy and a return to their old power and status. Thus Hippias could have had some potential support. Hippias' father, Pisistratus, had once made his return to power from exile by landing at Marathon (1.62).

ten generals   according to the Athenian constitution, the Athenian people elected ten generals each year to command their army. At a moment like this, all the generals were present together and they took it in turns to hold supreme command, the presidency, for a day. Military positions were filled by election although almost every other position was filled by lot.

Miltiades   a member of one of the great aristocratic families of Athens. His father, Cimon, had been driven into exile by Pisistratus, and Cimon, his son, was a major figure in Athenian politics and policy in the years after the Persian Wars.

6.105 The first thing the generals did, while they were still in the city, was to send a messenger to Sparta. His name was **Philippides**, an Athenian who was trained as a long-distance runner. Well, this is what Philippides himself said, and he also gave this account to the Athenians. When he was on **Mount Parthenion** above **Tegea**, **Pan** met him. His story was that Pan called out his name and told him to ask the Athenians why they paid him no regard: after all, he was a friend of the Athenians and had often helped them in the past, and would do so again. The Athenians believed this story and, when things went well for them, they founded a shrine for Pan at the foot of the Acropolis and, because of Pan's message, they appeased him with annual sacrifices and a torch-race.

This helmet is preserved at Olympia, one of the most important of the pan-Hellenic shrines and the site of the Olympic Games. On the helmet is inscribed 'Miltiades, dedicated to Zeus', and it is likely that Miltiades, the victor of Marathon, dedicated the helmet from that victory.

Philippides or Phidippides – both of the names appear in the manuscripts. Whatever his name, this is the real run of Marathon, not from Marathon to Athens, but from Athens to Sparta. Later versions had him getting back in time for the battle and then running with the news of victory to Athens and then, not surprisingly, dying. The first marathon of the modern era was run in 1896 and was 24 miles – 40,000 metres – long. However, the length of the current marathon is not that distance; it is 26 miles and 385 yards, the distance from Windsor Castle, near London, to the White City stadium, in London – the route of the marathon at the London Olympics of 1908. The 385 yards was added to ensure that the race finished in front of the royal box.

Mount Parthenion the mountain, 3,985 feet high, is in Arcadia. It is one of the roughest and most remote areas of the mountainous Peloponnese and stands above Tegea (see map on p. 9).

Tegea one of the most important city-states of the Peloponnese.

Pan a mountain god native to Arcadia, half goat half man, who brought *panic* to people. It has been suggested that high-altitude running can generate hallucinations; the playing of pan-pipes in the Andes has a similar effect. Perhaps this could account for the strange meeting. There is good archaeological evidence that a cult of Pan was established in Athens soon after the Persian Wars.

6.106   Anyway, this Philippides was sent by the generals on the mission when he said that Pan appeared to him, and he arrived in Sparta on the day after he left the city of Athens. When he got there, he spoke as follows to the **Spartan officials**: 'Spartans, the Athenians beg you to come to their aid. Do not allow **the most ancient city** in Greece to fall into slavery at the hands of the barbarians. Eretria has already been enslaved and Greece is the weaker by one important city.'

So Philippides delivered to the Spartans the message that he had been commanded to bring and they resolved to help. However, they could not do this at once because they did not want to **break the law; it was the ninth day of the month** and they said that they could not set out until the moon was full.

6.107   While the Spartans were waiting for the full moon, Hippias, the son of Pisistratus, was guiding the Persians to Marathon. On the night before, Hippias dreamed a dream in which he slept with his own mother. From this dream he drew the conclusion that he would return to Athens, regain his power and die, an old man, in his own country. This was the conclusion that he came to. Then he continued his guidance of the Persians. He settled those captured from Eretria on the island which belongs to the Styreans and is called Aigilia. Then he brought the fleet to Marathon. They landed there and he was marshalling the Persian forces as they disembarked. Whilst he was doing this he was seized by an unusual bout of coughing and sneezing. Since he was an old man, many of his teeth were loose anyway and one of them fell out with the force of his sneezing. The tooth fell onto the sand and he was desperate to find it. When he couldn't, he groaned and said to those standing around him, 'This is not our land and we will not be able to conquer it. My tooth has the only part of it that is mine.' Hippias concluded that his dream had been fulfilled in this way.

Spartan officials Philippides is likely to have spoken to the ephors, the governing magistrates of Sparta.

the most ancient city   this is not particularly tactful to the Spartans, who are Dorians. The Ionian Athenians claimed to be born of the soil of their own lands, so that they were the original and oldest inhabitants of Greece (see notes on 6.102 and 7.204).

break the law; it was the ninth day of the month   Herodotus' account doesn't make sense, not least because it suggests that the Spartans couldn't fight at the beginning of any month. It is likely that the reason for inaction is the festival of the Carnea (see note on 7.206). The Spartans were famous for their attention to religious festivals and divine guidance as the narrative of Thermopylae and their slowness to join battle at Plataea until the omens were right (9.61, p. 133) also show. Later in the fifth century this was still a key factor in making decisions (Thucydides 5.54, 75, 76). However, such reluctance also did look suspiciously like self-interest because the Spartans were always slow to leave Sparta and fight away from home.

The battle: 6.109–17, 120

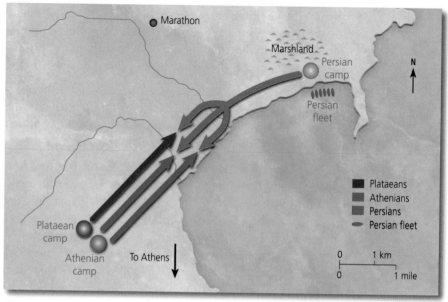

The position of the armies at the start of the battle of Marathon, 490 BC.

6.109   Amongst the Athenian generals **opinion on strategy was divided.** Some of them were against making an attack on the grounds that they were too few to attack the Persian army. Others, including Miltiades, were in favour of an attack. At this point, opinion was divided and the worse alternative was beginning to hold sway. In addition to the generals, there was an eleventh man, chosen by lot, who had the   5 right to vote, called the **polemarch.** In the distant past the Athenians had given the polemarch a vote equal to that of the generals. The polemarch at the time was Callimachus of **Aphidna**, and Miltiades now went to him and spoke.

---

opinion on strategy was divided   this is typical of the Greeks throughout the Persian Wars. In this case it is division amongst the Athenians. Later, it is disagreement between city-states, and it gets worse. Amongst the Greeks there are always differences of opinion which can make decision-making precarious.

polemarch   this is something of a muddle. The polemarch was originally the official responsible for the conduct of war, but the generalship at this time was a relatively new concept. Most scholars believe that the polemarch was supreme in 490 BC, but they also agree that by 487 BC the ten generals had assumed real authority. Thus, it may be no surprise that neither Herodotus' sources nor Herodotus are entirely clear on the exact situation in 490 BC. That lack of clarity would have been compounded by the descendants of these great men constructing versions of events favourable to the honour of their own family.

Aphidna   an Athenian would be identified by his name, often his father's name, but also by his deme, the area of Attica he came from. The 139 demes were a vital building block in the democratic constitution.

'It is up to you now, Callimachus. Either you will enslave Athens or you will set her free and leave a memory for all generations of men even greater than that of Harmodius and Aristogiton. For here and now the Athenians face the greatest danger in all of their history. If they bend under the yoke of the Medes, we have seen what they will suffer at the hands of Hippias. But if this city survives, it can be the **first in Greece**. How can this be and how can the outcome of events come down to you? I'll tell you now. The opinions of the ten generals are divided: some want to attack, others don't. If we don't attack, I expect that some terrible civil strife will fall upon Athens and destroy our principles and we shall go over to the Medes. However, if we do attack before any bad idea like this comes to any of the Athenians, we can prevail in battle as long as the gods deal fairly with us. And so, here and now, all of this is up to you. It depends on you. If you lend your support to my plan, your country is free and your city is the first in Greece. But if you choose the side of those who speak against attack, the very opposite of the good things I have described will come to pass.'

6.110   With these words Miltiades won over Callimachus, and, with the support of the polemarch, it was decided to engage the enemy. The position of **presidency** was held by a different general each day, and the generals who supported attack all offered the presidency to Miltiades. But he refused the offer and didn't make the attack until he held the presidency by right.

It is up to you now, Callimachus   no speech in an ancient historian's work is a transcript; here the speech is anachronistic in that it allows Miltiades to speak with remarkable foresight of the rest of the fifth century and the role of Athens in it.

Harmodius and Aristogiton   in the mythology of Athens, these two were the tyrannicides, the young men who put an end to the tyranny in 510 BC. In fact, they didn't kill Hippias, the ruling tyrant, but Hipparchus, his brother. The expulsion of Hippias was mainly due to the intervention of the Spartans. However, that was not particularly palatable to the Athenians, who gave a greater role to these young men. For a full account of their actions, see Thucydides 6.53–9. In that account Thucydides makes clear that the original cause of the dispute that led to the death of Hipparchus was his attempt to seduce Harmodius, who was Aristogiton's lover.

first in Greece   once again, Miltiades speaks with 20/20 foresight, seeing the major role that Athens will play in the fifth century after the victories at Marathon and Salamis.

presidency   Herodotus' account of the delay in fighting doesn't make sense in constitutional terms. There must have been better reasons, but perhaps Herodotus' sources didn't know them. One possibility is that they were waiting for the Spartans, but perhaps that fact would have undermined the glory of the moment. Perhaps Miltiades was waiting for an opportunity when the Persian cavalry could not operate. Perhaps they were waiting to see which side would blink first. The average hoplite certainly wouldn't have known, just as the D-Day soldier wouldn't have known of the thoughts of Eisenhower or Montgomery. Their first-hand accounts tell of the detailed and the personal, but little or nothing of the strategic factors.

6.111   And when the presidency did come to him, the Athenians took up their positions for the attack as follows. Callimachus, the polemarch, led the right wing – it was the law of the Athenians at that time that the polemarch should be in command of the right wing. After him, **the tribes followed on in their usual formation**, one after the other. The **Plataeans** were the last to take up their positions, holding the left wing. Ever since this battle, it has been the tradition at the sacrifices held in the **festival that takes place every four years** for the herald to pray for the prosperity not only of the Athenians but also of the Plataeans. And this was the formation of the Athenians at Marathon. The Athenian battle line was equal in length to the Persian battle line, but **the centre was only a few ranks deep** and it was here that it was at its weakest. However, both wings were strong in numbers.

Aristion the hoplite, dated c. 510 BC. This grave sculpture of an Athenian represented in hoplite armour was found at Velanideza in Attica. The soldier wears a helmet, breast plate over a pleated chiton, and greaves to protect his legs. He carries a hoplite spear. As well as the equipment mentioned above, each man generally carried a shield.

the tribes followed on in their usual formation   there were ten tribes in Athens, each named after a hero. They were an important part of the structure of Athenian society: they were the way of structuring the army, but they were also central to major constitutional features such as the Council of 500, and at the City Dionysia there were choral competitions between tribes.

Plataeans   Plataea is a small town in Boeotia (see map on p. 79) which sent 1,000 men, according to Cornelius Nepos, a first-century BC historian. The Athenians never forgot this help, commemorating it at the Great Panathenaea, their major festival (see below). Later, in 427, they also gave the Plataeans citizenship of Athens, a rare gesture.

festival that takes place every four years   this refers to the Great Panathenaea, the greatest festival in honour of Athena. At that festival a new robe was presented to the small wooden statue of Athena on the Acropolis, and it is that festival that is depicted on the frieze of the Parthenon (see Ian Jenkyns, *The Parthenon Frieze* (British Museum Press, 1994)).

the centre was only a few ranks deep   the hoplite phalanx, the shield-to-shield line of soldiers, usually formed up eight men deep (Thucydides 4.94, 6.67). The best estimates for numbers suggest that the Athenians and Plataeans in total were about 10,000 strong and the Persians were double that number. So the Athenian tactic of thinning the ranks was necessary to avoid being outflanked. A normal hoplite battle was a ferocious collision between two massed, heavily armed ranks, using a thrusting spear. Thereafter, it became an enormous pushing match, until one side turned and fled.

6.112 When they had taken up their positions and **the sacrificial omens were favourable**, the Athenians were let loose, and they charged against the Persians **at a run**. The distance between the two armies was not less than **eight stades**. When the Persians ⁴⁵

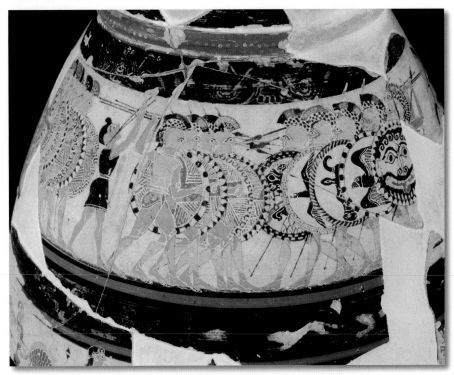

The Chigi Vase: this oinochoe, or wine-pourer, painted in Corinth in the third quarter of the seventh century BC, was found at Veii in Etruria. It shows a hoplite phalanx marching into battle to the sound of a pipe-player who kept the phalanx in step (see Thucydides 5.70).

the sacrificial omens were favourable   Greek battles had a certain ritual design and the inspection of the entrails of sacrificed animals was an important part of that. The nature of those omens was critical and did affect the timing of the battle (see the note on 9.62 at the battle of Plataea).

at a run, eight stades   it is hard, perhaps even impossible, to run in full hoplite armour at all, let alone a mile. But the run is part of the myth of the battle – like the little ships of Dunkirk or the Spitfires of the battle of Britain – and they probably closed quickly so that the Persian archers had less time to do them damage.

In 424 BC, 65 years later, the Marathon veterans are still going on about the battle in Aristophanes' comedy *Wasps* (lines 1077–85):

> Straightaway we ran out, with spear, with shield and fought against them, after drinking a draught of sharp bitter spirit. Each man stood beside the next, biting his lip with anger. Because of their arrows we could not see the sky but still, with the gods' help, towards evening we pushed them back. Then we pursued them, harpooning them through their baggy trousers, and they fled.

saw them attacking at a run, they prepared to meet the attack. They thought that the Athenians were possessed by madness, suicidal madness – they were few in number and were charging at a run **without the support of cavalry or archers.** That was the Persians' judgement of the matter but, when the Athenians engaged with the Persians in numbers, they fought heroically. They were the first Greeks 50 known to join battle with the enemy at a run and the first Greeks to face, without flinching, the **sight of Median dress** and the men wearing it. Until this moment the very word 'Mede' scared them.

6.113 The battle lasted a long time. In the centre the barbarians were victorious – that was where the Persians themselves and the **Sacae** were. Here the barbarians were 55 so successful that they broke the Athenian line and pursued them inland. But on both wings the Athenians and Plataeans were victorious. Although they were victorious here, they left the defeated enemy to flee. Instead they brought together the two successful wings against the Persians who had broken through in the middle, and defeated them. They pursued the fleeing Persians, cutting them down 60 until they reached the sea. At that point they called for fire and **took hold of the ships.**

6.114 It was at this moment that Callimachus, the polemarch, died a noble death. One of the generals, Stesilaus, the son of Thrasylaus, was also killed. **Cynegeiros**, the son of Euphorion, also perished. He **took hold of the stern of a ship** and his hand 65 was cut off with an axe. Many other famous Athenians also died.

---

without the support of cavalry or archers   these were the key elements in the Persian method of fighting, causing casualties either with swift attacks in the case of the cavalry or from a distance in the case of archers.

sight of Median dress   not true, in that the Ionians had fought the Persians for several years in the Ionian revolt.

Sacae   a people from the north of the Persian empire and some of Persia's best fighters.

took hold of the ships, took hold of the stern of a ship   these heroic scenes recall the battle at the ships in Homer's *Iliad* 15.704–46, where Hector reaches the Greek ships. It is also noticeable that Greek generals die in battle, now and throughout the fifth century: Datis and Artaphernes here and Xerxes later are at no such risk. Herodotus' battles end with details of the death of the great, presumably because of the survival of monuments in their memory.

Cynegeiros   the brother of Aeschylus, the tragedian and author of the *Persians,* the only surviving Greek play that deals with historical events (see the extract on pp. 116–18). Although Aeschylus wrote the *Oresteia*, a trilogy of plays that is the West's first great theatrical achievement, his epitaph only referred to the fact that he had fought at Marathon.

6.115   In this action the Athenians captured seven ships, but the barbarians put to sea with the others, picked up the Eretrian slaves from the island where they had left them and sailed around **Cape Sounion**. Their plan was to get to Athens before the Athenians. Amongst the Athenians some charged the **Alcmaeonids** with responsibility for this: they said that they had made a deal with the Persians and had given a signal with a shield to the Persians when they were on their ships.   70

6.116   So the Persians sailed round Sounion. The Athenians came to the defence of the city with all speed and got there before the Persians. Their camp at Marathon was in a place sacred to **Heracles** and, on their return, they set up their camp on another site sacred to Heracles in Cynosarges. The barbarians' fleet lay off **Phaleron** – at that time the harbour of Athens – but it made no move against Athens and then they sailed back to Asia.   75

6.117   In the battle at Marathon **about 6,400 barbarians and 192 Athenians died**. This was the number of casualties on both sides. In the battle an extraordinary thing happened. The story goes that an Athenian, Epizelos, the son of Couphagoras,   80

Cape Sounion   this is the south-east tip of Attica where the Athenians built a temple to Poseidon at about the same time they built the Parthenon.

Alcmaeonids   one of the greatest, and certainly richest, of Athenian families. For an account of Alcmaeon and the source of the family's wealth, see 6.125. Pericles, the most important political figure in fifth-century Athens, was a member of the family. However, in these times they were suspected of sympathies with the deposed tyrant, Hippias, and hence with the enemy. Megacles, an Alcmaeonid, came to marry the daughter of Cleisthenes, the tyrant of Sicyon. The story of how is one of the very best in Herodotus (6.125–30).

Heracles   a hero whose twelve labours brought him the unique reward of being accepted as a god. Although he was a god particularly favoured by the Dorian Greeks, he was widely worshipped.

Phaleron   a flat beach eight miles from Athens, used at this time as the Athenians' harbour. However, when the size and significance of the fleet increased, they moved to the enclosed harbour of Piraeus.

about 6,400 barbarians and 192 Athenians died   these figures are a long way from the millions Herodotus speaks of when recounting the invasion of 480 BC. The numbers and the difference between them are feasible. The Athenian figure is likely to be right: the funeral mound recorded the names of the dead (Pausanias 1.32) and it may even be that the number of 192 is reflected in the number of figures on the Parthenon frieze. As for the Persians, the side that is routed is bound to take heavy casualties in flight. So 6,400 could be right. Callimachus had vowed to Artemis a kid for every Persian killed and Xenophon (*Anabasis* 3.2.12) tells us that the Athenians had to pay her in instalments, 500 each year. Plutarch, writing in the second century AD with a passionate hostility to Herodotus, says that the Persian dead were beyond counting and the figure of 6,400 demeans the achievement of the Athenians (*The Malice of Herodotus* 862b).

whilst fighting heroically in close combat, lost his sight, even though he was not struck or wounded. From that moment he remained blind for the rest of his life. I have heard his account and he said that a great warrior seemed to face him, and his beard overshadowed his whole shield. But the phantom passed him by and killed the next man. I have heard that this was his account of what happened.

6.120 Two thousand Spartans came to Athens after the full moon. Such was their desire to be there that they arrived in Athens on the third day after their departure from Sparta. Even though they arrived too late for the battle, they were desperate to see the Persians, so they went to Marathon to have a look. And after they had praised the Athenians for what they had done, they went back home again.

---

1 What aspects of the story does Herodotus concentrate on and why? Is he successful in creating an exciting narrative?

2 What sources would have been available to Herodotus? How does that have an impact on the nature of his narrative?

3 What are the limitations of Herodotus' account?

4 'The greatness of the victory is gone. The climax of the famous exploit has come to nothing. No fight, no great action seems to have happened at all, just a brief clash with the Persians after their landing' (Plutarch). Is this a fair criticism of Herodotus' account?

5 What is the role of Miltiades' speech in this story? Is such a speech justifiable in Herodotus' work?

6 How does this narrative compare with oral accounts of any modern war?

7 The poet Robert Graves wrote in his poem *The Persian Version*:
   Truth-loving Persians do not dwell upon
   The trivial skirmish fought near Marathon.
   What might a Persian account of the battle of Marathon be like?

8 With what other battles in history can Marathon be compared as an embodiment of a nation's identity? What impact does that aspect have on the narrative?

9 John Stuart Mill said that the battle of Marathon was more important in British history than the battle of Hastings. What reasons could there be for such a judgement?

---

5 The coming of the Persian invasion

After the defeat at Marathon, Darius was eager to take immediate revenge on the Athenians. Herodotus tells us (7.1) that he spent three years making preparations. However, revolt in Egypt distracted him from his purpose and in 486 BC he died.

Herodotus gives a substantial amount of time and coverage to the decision of Darius' son, Xerxes, to invade Greece, the preparations of the army and the journey to Greece. This gives an insight into the character of Xerxes, the enormity of the expedition and the difficulty of decision-making.

The decision to invade Greece: 7.5–18

7.5　**When Darius died**, the kingdom passed to his son, Xerxes. In the beginning, Xerxes himself had no desire to launch an expedition against Greece, but he gathered his forces for an attack on Egypt. At that time **Mardonius, the son of Gobryas,** Xerxes' cousin and the son of Darius' sister, held the most influence over Xerxes. He kept on making the same proposal: 'My lord,' he said, 'it is not right 5 that the Athenians, who have caused the Persians such great harm, should not pay for what they have done. As for now, you should carry on with what you have in hand, but once you have subdued the arrogance of Egypt, make your expedition against Athens. In that way you will gain a great reputation amongst men and, in future, people will think twice about attacking your land.' 10

When Darius died Darius' greatest achievement wasn't conquest, whatever Xerxes may say later, but the creation of a structure of administration for the Persian empire (see 3.89–97).

Mardonius, the son of Gobryas Mardonius was not only connected to Xerxes in the way Herodotus describes, but he also married Darius' daughter. His father, Gobryas, had been one of the seven conspirators who had overthrown Smerdis the Magus and put Darius on the throne (3.70–9). He was also Darius' key adviser on the invasion of Scythia (4.132, 134). He was, therefore, immensely well connected and he was responsible for the early, and unsuccessful, mission of 490 BC. His fleet was very badly damaged going round Mount Athos (6.43–4) and, after this failure, Mardonius was relieved of his command (6.94), so that others led the attack on Athens in 490. However, his time will come again in that he is the leader of the Persian forces that stay behind in 479.

This was his plea for vengeance, but he also always added that **Europe was a very beautiful place**, excellent in its quality, producing cultivated trees of all kinds: it was such a country that, of all men, only the king of Persia was fit to possess it, he said.

7.6   Mardonius kept on saying this because he was always eager for a new challenge and because he wanted to be the governor of Greece. In the end, he got his way and persuaded Xerxes to do what he said. There were also other factors that contributed to persuading Xerxes. First, messengers had come from the **Aleuadai** – they were the kings of Thessaly – to say that they were deeply committed to an invasion of Greece. Secondly, the **Pisistratids** who had come to **Susa** kept on saying the same things as the Aleuadai, but were offering yet further inducements. For

Part of a relief from the northern stairs of the Apadana at Persepolis, but later moved to the Treasury. The seated king Darius holds a lotus flower, a royal prerogative, and is greeted by an official, perhaps Pharnaces, the mayor of the palace. In the middle are two incense burners.

Europe was a very beautiful place   Mardonius isn't telling the truth about the nature of Greece. The Persians were particularly keen on the cultivation of trees and gardens (see 7.31, where Xerxes gives great honour to a plane tree).

Aleuadai   Thessaly is in northern Greece, a mountainous region, the land of Mount Ossa and Mount Olympus. The Aleuadai were strong supporters of Persia (7.172, 9.1) and presumably hoped to secure their power in the region through Persian support.

Pisistratids   the deposed and exiled family of tyrants from Athens. Hippias accompanied the expedition in 490 BC (see 6.102, 107, 109 on pp. 39, 41 and 43), and the family are still there a few years later, hoping to be reinstated by the Persians.

Susa   about 150 miles east of the river Tigris and 150 miles north of the Persian Gulf (see map on p. 1). It was a very ancient site, first occupied c. 7000 BC, and Darius made it the most important centre of administration for his empire. This is reflected in the fact that Susa was the end of the Royal Road (see 5.52–3). The Persian court spent part of each year in Susa and Darius undertook a major building programme there. The frieze of the Immortals (see p. 87) was found there and Aeschylus' *Persians* (see extract on pp. 116–18) was set there.

they had come to Susa with **Onomacritus**, who was an Athenian oracle-monger and interpreter of the prophecies of **Musaeus**. He had come with them so that he might see the Persian king, and so, whenever the Pisistratids were paying grand compliments to the king, he would recite his oracles. If there was anything that was negative for the Persians, he didn't mention it, but he would always catalogue the most favourable things, saying that it was fated that the Hellespont should be yoked by a Persian, and in that way describing the route of the expedition. So, he was applying pressure with his oracles and the Pisistratids and the Aleuadai were doing the same by **presenting their proposals**.

7.7   When Xerxes had been persuaded to attack Greece, the first thing he did, in the year after Darius' death, was make an attack on those who had revolted in Egypt. He defeated them and reduced the whole of Egypt to a state of greater slavery than it had suffered under Darius. He put Achaemenes, his brother and the son of Darius, in charge of the country. Some time later, during his period of rule, Achaemenes was murdered by Inarus, the son of Psammetichus, a Libyan.

7.8   After his conquest of Egypt, Xerxes' intention was to lead his army against Athens. He called a meeting of a select group of Persian nobles to hear their opinions and tell all of them what he wanted to do. When they were gathered, Xerxes spoke as follows. 'Men of Persia, I will not be bringing to you **a new way of being**. Rather, I will be following the ways that I have inherited. As my elders have told me, it has never been our way to live a quiet life, ever since we took this empire from the Medes, when Cyrus succeeded Astyages. A god leads us on and, as we follow, much turns to our advantage. You all know **the great deeds of Cyrus and Cambyses and my father, Darius**, and their conquest of other peoples. There is

---

Onomacritus, Musaeus Musaeus was a mythical singer, originally from Eleusis and closely linked to Orpheus. Among his works are oracles and these were collected around 500 BC by Onomacritus, who was expelled from Athens for forging an oracle.

presenting their proposals Xerxes is beset by many different voices with different motives. Decision-making is not easy at such a time and Herodotus is trying to convey the complexity of human motives and the difficulty of making a decision.

a new way of being, the great deeds of Cyrus and Cambyses and my father, Darius Xerxes is very keen to ensure that his actions are seen as part of the ancient tradition of his predecessors who extended the power of the Persian empire. Cyrus (559–530 BC) defeated Croesus (546 BC, 1.84–6) and the Ionian Greeks (1.157–76) and captured Babylon (539 BC, 1.178–91). Cambyses (530–522 BC) conquered Egypt, and Darius (522–486 BC) extended Persian power yet further, to India, and also attacked Greece. However, there is irony in Xerxes' use of these models. Cyrus was defeated and killed by the Massagetae, a people who lived north of the Persian empire to the east of the Caspian Sea. His fate was to have his head put in a wineskin full of human blood by Queen Tomyris (1.214). Cambyses was judged by Herodotus to have gone mad in Egypt and died at a time when there was a coup taking place against him (3.66). And, of course, Darius' attack on Athens in 490 BC failed. The model of Xerxes' forebears is not encouraging; Xerxes actually does need to find a new way of being.

no point in telling you things that you all know. As for me, since I came to this 45
throne, I have been thinking how I might not fall short of the deeds of the past
in winning honour and be no less successful in gaining power for the Persians.
In my thinking, I have a plan that will bring to us glory and a country that is not
smaller or **poorer** than the one we now have. Rather, it is richer. Furthermore, we
will gain **revenge and recompense**. For this reason I have gathered you together 50
here to share with you what I intend to do. My plan is to bridge the Hellespont
and take an expedition through Europe into Greece. Our purpose will be to take
revenge on the Athenians for all that they did to the Persians and my father. You
have seen for yourselves that Darius was eager to make an expedition against these
people. He died and it was not granted to him to take his revenge. I, however, will 55
not cease from my efforts on behalf of Darius and the other Persians until I have
captured Athens and burnt it to the ground. For it was the Athenians who were
the first to wrong me and my father.

Darius started the building of the great palace complex at Persepolis in 515 BC, and work was continued by Xerxes. The largest and most significant building was the Apadana (visible with long columns in the background), used for official audiences. It was 69 metres square and had 72 columns, each 19 metres high.

poorer Xerxes is making Greece into something that it isn't, presumably under the influence of Mardonius' opinion. Greece is not a rich country and Herodotus' work continually emphasizes that it is a hard, poor one (see Demaratus' comment in 7.102 (p. 75) and the scene at Mardonius' tent in 9.82 (pp. 141–2)).

revenge and recompense Xerxes sought to punish the mainland Greeks for their involvement in the Ionian revolt (499–494 BC) and to make up for the Persian defeat at Marathon (490 BC). His range of motives is very similar to those of Croesus in his attack on Cappadocia (1.73). The different reasons for conquest can lead to confusion in the war itself, as the invasion of Iraq in 2003 shows.

'The first thing they did was come to Sardis with **Aristagoras of Miletus**, our slave, and burn our sacred groves and sanctuaries. Then I am sure you all know 60 what they did to our force that landed in Greece under the command of Datis and Artaphernes. For these two reasons, I am ready to make an expedition against the Athenians and, furthermore, I have come to the conclusion that there are many advantages in such a plan. If we conquer these people and their neighbours, who live in the land of **Pelops the Phrygian,** we will create a Persian kingdom that will 65 match **Zeus' heaven. For the sun will look down on no land other than our own.** With you, I will make all lands into one country, passing over all of Europe. My enquiries tell me that this is the way things are: no city, no people will be left able to face us in battle, once we have eliminated those I have listed. In this way both the guilty and the innocent will bear our **yoke of slavery.** 70

'You can please me by doing as follows. Whenever I declare to you that it is time for us to come together, you must all attend with all eagerness. To the man who comes with his army **most finely equipped**, I will give rewards that are the most

---

Aristagoras of Miletus   Aristagoras was the chief instigator of the Ionian revolt, in which the Greek-speaking city-states rose up against Persian rule. He came to Sparta and Athens in search of support (5.49–51, 97). The Spartans refused to help, the Athenians didn't. Herodotus describes the Ionian revolt in 5.28–6.33.

Pelops the Phrygian   Xerxes means the Spartans and the Peloponnese, i.e. literally the island of Pelops. The story was told that Pelops originally came from Phrygia in the south of Ionia. However, the rest of Pelops' career is more interesting: he was the son of Tantalus, who served him up as a meal to the gods. Demeter ate his shoulder by mistake and he was given an ivory replacement. He was the father of Atreus and, therefore, the grandfather of Agamemnon and Menelaus.

Herodotus gives Xerxes the perspective of a man from the East in making him refer to Pelops as 'the Phrygian' and ignoring all the mythical elements. This might also encourage him to think that he is not the first man from the East to rule Greece.

Zeus' heaven   Persian kings normally invoke the gods of Zoroastrianism, whose chief divinity is Ahura Mazda: compare the importance of Ahura Mazda in the Bisitun inscription (see pp. 76–7). Although Herodotus is sensitive to the differences between religions and cultures, he chooses here to equate Ahura Mazda with Zeus.

the sun will look down on no land other than our own   it seems that all empires run the risk of thinking and talking in this way. Jupiter says of the Roman empire, 'imperium sine fine dedi', 'I have given empire without end' (Virgil, *Aeneid* 1.279) and the British spoke of the empire 'on which the sun never set'.

yoke of slavery   the Persians are presented as a people whose imperial purpose is enslavement. This is contrasted with the freedom of the Greeks.

most finely equipped   one of the key features of Herodotus' account is that the Persian army is an object of display, much to be admired and inspected. The Greek army is not so pretty, and Herodotus' account explores the difference between appearance and reality.

prized in our country. This, therefore, is what we must do, but I wouldn't want you to think that this is only my own, personal plan. I am bringing the matter forward 75 for open debate. **I command any of you who wants** to express his opinion to do so now.'

7.9 That was the end of Xerxes' speech, and after him Mardonius spoke. 'My lord, **you are the best of all the Persians,** not only those of the past, but also those of the future. Everything you have said is **full of wisdom and truth**, but I congratulate 80 you particularly on not allowing the Ionians, those who dwell in Europe, to treat us with scorn. They are worthless. Look at the **Sacae and the Indians and the Ethiopians and the Assyrians** and all the many other great tribes. They did the Persians no wrong, but we defeated them because **we wanted to extend our empire.** It would be terrible if we held all of them as our slaves, but do not take our 85 revenge on the Greeks who were the first to do us wrong. What are we afraid of? Their **numbers?** Their **financial strength?** We know about their way of fighting. We know that they are weak. We have conquered their children and hold them in our power, for 'their children' is what the **Ionians and Aeolians and Dorians** call those who have settled in our country. I know what they are like from **personal** 90 **experience.** I campaigned against these men under your father's orders. We had advanced as far as Macedon and nearly got to Athens itself and no one came

---

I command any of you who wants   here lies the paradox. Xerxes wants his advisers to say what they think, but he has already told them his decision. Once again the contrast is with Greek ways, the land of debate and, in the case of Athens, democracy. Amongst the Greeks there is no single absolute power, so they debate and disagree.

you are the best of all the Persians, full of wisdom and truth   Mardonius embodies the threat of idle flattery. He is a man of high position who has recently failed, so that he is desperate to win approval from the new king.

Sacae and the Indians and the Ethiopians and the Assyrians   the Persians never did manage to take control of these extremities of empire (see 3.93–4, 97–8, 101 (p. 34)). Mardonius is exaggerating previous success.

we wanted to extend our empire   this debate does raise the question of why empires need to keep on expanding.

numbers, financial strength   it is typical of the Persians that Mardonius thinks that these are the only things that matter.

Ionians and Aeolians and Dorians   three ethnic groups into which the Greeks are divided. For Ionians and Dorians, see note on 6.102. The Aeolians were a third group, who came originally from Boeotia and Thessaly and settled on Lesbos and the northern coast of Ionia.

personal experience   Mardonius' account of his own failed campaign against Greece is highly selective. Indeed, it bears no resemblance at all to Herodotus' narrative (6.43–5).

out to face us in battle. There's something else, too. The **Greek way of fighting**, as I know, is the most ill-conceived it could be. It's a product of ignorance and stupidity. Whenever they declare war on each other, they find the best and flattest 95 piece of ground and both sides turn up and fight, so that even the winners depart with serious losses. As for the losers, well, I don't know where to start; they are completely wiped out. This is what they should do, since they all speak the same language. They should make use of their heralds and messengers and settle their differences by any means other than battle. If they really must fight against each 100 other, they should find a place where it is very hard for each side to beat the other and have their trial of strength there.

'So you can see that the Greek method isn't a very good one and that is why I got as far as Macedon and they didn't give any thought of fighting. My lord, who is going to oppose your invasion, which will bring multitudes from Asia and all 105 your ships? In my opinion, the Greeks are not going to show that much courage. If I were to be proved wrong and they, driven by folly, were to come against us in battle, they would learn that we are the best men in all the world in war. **We must try everything.** Nothing happens of its own accord, but everything comes to men from having a go.' 110

7.10 Mardonius ended his speech at this point, having done all he could to make Xerxes' decision look a good one. **All the other Persians remained silent**, not daring to express an opinion contrary to the one that had been put forward. However, **Artabanus**, the son of Hystaspes, who relied on the fact that he was Xerxes' uncle,

---

Greek way of fighting Mardonius is right in his account of the nature of Greek warfare, battles enacted on the flat plains. However, the Greeks were neither stupid nor poor fighters. They fought on the plains because those are the rare and valuable fertile areas of Greece. Also, the land-battles of the Persian Wars proved that their weaponry, training and courage made them formidable opponents. There is a rich irony in that Mardonius commands the Persian forces that are defeated on land at Plataea in 479 BC.

We must try everything Mardonius speaks the words of an empire's ambition. However, Herodotus has already told us that all Mardonius really wants is a personal position for himself as governor of Greece (7.6, p. 50).

All the other Persians remained silent once again, the problems of a Persian debate. Are they silent out of agreement or fear of disagreeing? Only Artabanus has the experience and the position to be able to disagree, even though Mardonius' speech is a fabrication.

Artabanus he is one of the key figures in the whole narrative. He is older and more experienced than Xerxes and he alone has the status, as Darius' brother, to tell the truth and disagree. In tragedy there is often the figure of the 'tragic warner', the man who can see the truth who is ignored until it is too late. Artabanus fulfils that role for the Persians.

7.10a made the following speech. 'My lord, **unless both sides of the argument are** **115** **expressed**, it is not possible to choose the better one. All you can do is follow the opinion that has been expressed. However, just as we don't **identify pure gold** on its own, but by rubbing it against other gold, so, when both arguments have been expressed, we can identify the better one. I told your father and my brother, Darius, not to **attack the Scythians**, since they were a people who didn't have a **120** single city anywhere. However, he hoped to conquer these Scythian nomads, so he didn't listen to my advice. He invaded their country and, when he returned, his army had suffered the loss of many fine men.

'You, my lord, are about to make an attack on men who are much better than the Scythians, a people who are said to be the best **on sea and on land**. There is danger **125**
7.10b here, and it is only right that I should tell you so. You say that you are going to bridge the Hellespont and lead your army across Europe to Greece. You could be defeated on land or on sea or on both. They are said to be men of great bravery, and it is possible to measure that bravery: when Datis and Artaphernes took such a massive force to Attica, the Athenians defeated them all on their own. **130**

'Suppose things don't go so well on land and sea. If they attack us with their fleet, defeat us in a sea battle, sail to the Hellespont and break down the bridge, that
7.10c would be a real threat to us. I don't make these calculations based on any great personal wisdom, but we were very close to a disaster when your father yoked the Thracian Bosporus, built a bridge over the river Danube and crossed it to fight the **135** Scythians. At that time all sorts of Scythians were telling the Ionians to break the bridge, because the Ionians had been entrusted with guarding it. At that moment,

---

unless both sides of the argument are expressed Artabanus begins with words that could come from a sophist, one of the professional teachers of rhetoric and philosophy who thrived in Athens in the second half of the fifth century BC. The most renowned of these was Protagoras of Abdera (a city in Thrace, see map on p. 9), who was famous for saying that there were arguments on both sides of any question.

identify pure gold another of Artabanus' traits is his use of analogy: compare the reference to the trees (7.10e, p. 57) and the sea (7.16, p. 60). He does have a distinctive voice and character.

attack the Scythians Artabanus warned Darius against the invasion of Scythia (4.83). The narrative of the invasion of Scythia (4.89–142), a land populated by nomadic tribes, shows that the Persians came very close to disaster.

on sea and on land Artabanus is allowed to foresee the courage of the Greeks and their victories on both land and sea. Also, after Salamis the Persians were deeply worried that the bridge over the Hellespont might be destroyed (8.97).

if **Histiaeus, the tyrant of Miletus,** had supported the view of the other tyrants and not stood out against them, Persia would have been ruined. It is a terrible thing to hear it said that all of the king's future lay in the hands of one man. 140

7.10d 'Don't think about taking such a risk when there is no need to do so. Just listen to me. Dissolve this gathering. Do some thinking on your own and, whenever you are ready, tell us what you think is the best plan. I have found that **good planning** is the most valuable thing of all. Even if things then go against you, that does not mean that it is any less of a good plan. It is just that your plan has been beaten by 145 **chance**. If, however, you plan badly, even if chance is on your side and you have a

7.10e bit of luck, nevertheless you have still planned badly. You see how god strikes with his thunderbolt **the tallest trees** and doesn't allow them to show off. Little things don't bother him at all. You see how his bolts fall on the biggest houses and trees. It is god's way to keep in check things that are excessive. In just the same way, a 150 great army can be destroyed by a small one. When a god resents such people, he casts fear and thunder on them and they are shamefully destroyed. God doesn't

7.10f like **anyone else to have big ideas** other than himself. In all things haste brings mistakes and the price you pay is a great one. There is virtue in waiting; even if

7.10g that is not obvious immediately, in time you will find it to be so. That is my advice 155 to you, my king.

'As for you, son of Gobryas, stop talking this idle nonsense about the Greeks. They do not deserve to be talked about in such stupid terms. By insulting the Greeks you encourage the king himself to launch an invasion. I suggest that this is where you get all your enthusiasm from. It should not be that way. Slander is a terrible 160 thing, in that two men do wrong and one is wronged. The slanderer wrongs a man who isn't there, making accusations against him. The listener does wrong by believing what he hears before he knows the facts for sure. The man who isn't there is wronged in two ways: he is abused by one of the two and thought of as an evil man by the other. 165

Histiaeus, the tyrant of Miletus   many cities in Ionia were ruled by tyrants who owed their position to the support of the Persian king. These tyrants were left to guard the bridge over the Danube when Darius crossed to conduct his Scythian campaign. The deal was that, if Darius did not return after 60 days, they would dismantle the bridge. When the time came Histiaeus persuaded the other tyrants not to do this, so that Darius and his army were saved (4.137). Thereafter, Histiaeus was treated as a trusted adviser by Darius, but he was also suspected of contributing to the Ionian revolt. In the end he was captured and impaled by Artaphernes, the governor of Sardis (6.30).

good planning, chance, the tallest trees, anyone else to have big ideas   Artabanus deals in this part of his speech with many issues that concerned Greek thinkers in the fifth century: the power of reason and planning, the role of chance, the danger of greatness and the hostility of the gods to human excess. He also reminds us of the wisdom of Croesus at the very beginning of the work.

7.10h 'If you really must make an expedition against these people, let the king stay at home among his own people and we will both risk the lives of our own children. You, Mardonius, take command. Choose the men you want and take as big an army as you choose. If, as you say, all goes well for the king, let my children be killed, and me as well. If, however, things turn out as I say, let your children suffer   170 the same fate and you, too, if you get back home.

'If, however, you are unwilling to take this on, but you are still going to lead an army against Greece, I tell you that word of Mardonius will come to those who have been left behind here; it will say that Mardonius has brought great evil to the Persians, that he is being dragged about by dogs, somewhere in the land of   175 the Athenians or the Spartans. That is if it doesn't happen to him first on the journey. You will come to know what kind of men you are encouraging the king to attack.'

7.11 This was Artabanus' speech. **Xerxes was furious.** 'Artabanus,' he replied, 'you are the brother of my father. That will save you from the punishment that your words   180 of folly deserve. Nevertheless, you will suffer this disgrace for your cowardice: you will not accompany me on the campaign against Greece. Instead, **you will stay here with the women.** I will bring to completion without you all that I have said. **May I not be the son of Darius**, the son of Hystaspes, the son of Arsames, the son of Ariaramnes, the son of Teispes, the son of Achaemenes if I do not take   185 revenge on the Athenians. I know only too well that, even if we want to live in peace, they do not. They will come and invade our country if we are to judge from their actions in the past when they set fire to Sardis and made an expedition into Asia. **Retreat is not possible for either side.** This is how it is: we either act or we suffer, so that either this land falls under the rule of the Greeks or all of their land   190

Xerxes was furious   Xerxes' response is like that of Oedipus in Sophocles' *Oedipus the King* or Creon in Sophocles' *Antigone*, not allowing anyone else's voice to be heard. It is no surprise that the others present had kept silent.

you will stay here with the women   in the end Xerxes goes back on this decision, although he does send him home before the expedition comes to battle (7.53, p. 73).

May I not be the son of Darius   Xerxes reverts to the dynastic rhetoric of 7.8 (pp. 51–2) and the Bisitun inscription (see pp. 76–7).

Retreat is not possible for either side   Xerxes is also trapped inside the imperial notion that empire requires continual expansion to safeguard against attack. It is not likely that the Greeks would have moved against Persia in the fifth century BC. It took until the end of the fourth century BC for a Macedonian, Alexander, to threaten and conquer Persia. These words have worrying resonance throughout history – expansion justified as self-defence.

falls under our rule. There is no middle ground in our enmity. The noble thing for us, who have suffered already, is to take revenge now and in that way I will find out what terrible thing I am to suffer if I invade these people, these people whom **Pelops the Phrygian, the slave of my fathers**, conquered so utterly that even to this day these people and their land take their name from the man who conquered them.' 195

7.12   That was where the talking ended but later, when night was coming on, Artabanus' words began to gnaw at Xerxes. That night he gave the matter some thought and came to the firm conclusion that it wasn't the right thing for him to invade Greece. When he had made this decision, he fell asleep and during the night he 200 had the following **dream**, or that's what the Persians say. A man of great stature and beauty appeared to Xerxes and said, 'So, Persian, you're changing your mind, I see. You're not going to invade Greece, even though you've told the Persians to assemble an army. It's not a good thing to change your mind, and no one will forgive you. Follow the path you decided on during the day.' According to Xerxes, 205 the figure said this and flew away.

7.13   In the light of day Xerxes paid no attention to this dream. He summoned the Persians he had gathered before and said, 'Men of Persia, forgive me that I am so fickle in my plans. I have not yet reached the height of my mental powers and those who advised me to do this have been on at me all the time. When I 210 first heard Artabanus' opinion, **my youthfulness** boiled over straightaway and I poured forth words that were inappropriate, not the kind of thing you should say to your elders. But now I agree with him and I am going to follow his plan. So I've changed my mind and decided not to invade Greece. You can live a life of peace and quiet.' 215

Pelops the Phrygian, the slave of my fathers Xerxes returns to the rhetoric of 7.8 (pp. 51–3): it is not easy to see how Pelops was a slave of Xerxes' ancestors, except that Phrygia did come under Persian control.

dream   the Greeks believed that the gods communicated with men in a variety of ways: through sacrificial victims, through oracles, through signs and through dreams. From Homer onwards dreams are treated as significant (Homer *Iliad* 1.62–7, 148–51). In 1.107–8 the dreams that come to Astyages convince him that his daughter's son, Cyrus, will be a threat to him and, on that basis, he sets out to kill him. Similarly in 5.55–6 Hipparchus, the brother of Hippias, the tyrant of Athens, dreamt of his own death. Hipparchus consulted interpreters of dreams for an explanation.

my youthfulness   Herodotus sets up tension between the youth of Xerxes, a king new to power, the wisdom of the experienced Artabanus, and the threat of flattery of such a young king by Mardonius. In fact, Xerxes was born in c. 519 BC, so that at this time he would have been in his thirties.

When they heard this, the Persians prostrated themselves before him, **delighted by the decision**.

7.14   When night came, the same vision came again to the sleeping Xerxes. It stood by him and said, 'Son of Darius, now it seems that you have told the Persians to call off the expedition, paying no attention to my words, as if you heard them from a 220 nobody. Now, understand this. If you don't launch your expedition at once, this is what's going to happen. You became great and powerful in a short time. You will become a nobody again just as quickly.'

7.15   Xerxes was terrified by the vision. He leapt out of bed and sent a messenger to fetch Artabanus. When he arrived, Xerxes said to him, 'Artabanus, I wasn't in my 225 right mind in the first instance when I responded to your good advice with words of folly. However, a short time later I changed my mind and realized that I should do what you advised. Now I can't do it, even though I want to. Now I have done my about-turn and changed my mind, some dream appears and haunts me. Its advice is that I should not do this. And now it has made a threat and disappeared. 230 If it is a god that sends this thing and it is truly pleasing to him that this expedition should go against Greece, this same vision will appear to you and will give you the same order as it gives to me. I reckon that this is likely to happen if you take all my clothes and put them on, sit on my throne and then sleep in my bed.'

7.16   This is what Xerxes said to Artabanus, but at first Artabanus didn't want to obey 235 this order – he didn't think it right to sit on the royal throne. However, in the end he was forced to do as he was told, but not before he said, 'My lord, it is my opinion that it is all the same whether you have a good idea yourself or you are willing to listen to someone else who talks sense. In your case, you are capable of both, but you keep the company of bad men and that trips you up. It's the 240 same with **what men say about the sea**. In itself the sea is the most useful of all things to mankind, but blasts of wind fall upon it and do not allow it to be itself. When you insulted me, it wasn't that I was hurt personally. Rather it was this. **Two different proposals** were placed before the Persians: one would increase our

---

delighted by the decision   these are the same Persians who expressed no dissent when Xerxes announced his intention to invade Greece. Their silence did not signify consent.

what men say about the sea   this is the third such natural analogy that Artabanus has used (see 7.10a (p. 56) for the reference to gold and 7.10e (p. 57) for the reference to tall trees).

Two different proposals, two proposals   the repetition of 'two proposals' reflects an unusual moment of clumsiness in Herodotus' writing, perhaps suggesting Artabanus' own uncertainty.

arrogant destructiveness and the other would reduce it and tell us that it was a   245
bad thing to teach the soul always to want to have more than it has. And when
those **two proposals** were before us, you chose the one that was more dangerous
for you and for the Persians.

'So now, when you have turned to the better course and say that you are giving up
on the expedition against the Greeks, a dream comes to haunt you, sent by some   250
god, and won't allow you to disband the expedition. **My boy, these things do not
come from the gods.** I will tell you the nature of these dreams that come wandering
into the heads of men. After all, I'm much older than you. These visions in dreams
most often arise from the concerns of the day. We have been deeply involved with
this expedition in the days before now. If this thing is not as I surmise, but really   255
has something divine in it, you yourself have summed up the whole thing in what
you said. Let it appear to me, as it has appeared to you, and tell me what to do.
However, there is no reason why it should be more likely to appear to me dressed
in your clothes rather than my own, sleeping in your bed or in my own, if it wants
to appear anyway. After all, this thing, whatever it is that appears to you in your   260
sleep, isn't going to be so stupid as to see me and think that I'm you on the basis
of my wearing your clothes. What we must discover now is whether it thinks that
I am of no account and so will decide not to appear, whether I am wearing your
clothes or my own, but will still appear to you. If it does appear regularly, then I
would have to say that **it is of divine origin.** But if you have decided that this is   265
the way it's going to be and you are not going to be deflected from your purpose,
I'll have to sleep in your bed. So be it. I'll fulfil all the conditions you ask. Then let
it appear to me, too. Until then, I'll stick with my existing opinion.'

---

arrogant destructiveness   here Artabanus uses the word *hubris*, a key concept in Greek
morality, referring to human trespass onto divine territory. The danger is that power can
generate excess and a lack of respect for the order of things and man's place in the world.
Such *hubris* runs the risk of divine anger and then divine retribution, *nemesis*.

My boy, these things do not come from the gods   Artabanus' tone here to the king
of Persia is striking in that he addresses him as 'My boy' not 'My lord', which is normal.
Artabanus here introduces some of the rationality of the fifth century into the area of
divine revelation. Empedocles of Acragas in Sicily (*c.* 492–432 BC) gave a scientific account
of dreams; Hippocrates, the most famous physician of ancient times, who lived in the
second half of the fifth century BC, explained them as disturbances of the brain and
Democritus of Abdera in Thrace (born *c.* 460 BC) said that images penetrated the body
and emerged as dreams.

it is of divine origin   Artabanus may rehearse the rational arguments about dreams, but
in the end even he cannot break free of the belief in their divine origin.

7.17 Artabanus said this and did as he was told in the expectation that he would show that Xerxes was talking nonsense. He put on Xerxes' clothes and sat on the royal throne and later went to bed. As he slept, there came to him the same dream as had appeared to Xerxes. It stood over Artabanus and said, 'I suppose you're the one who is discouraging Xerxes from making an expedition against Greece, as if you were concerned for his welfare. Neither now nor in the future will you escape punishment for trying **to turn aside the inevitable**, and it has been made clear to Xerxes himself what must happen, if he is disobedient.' 270 275

7.18 According to Artabanus, the apparition made these threats and was about to burn out his eyes with red-hot iron bars. But he shouted out loud, jumped out of bed and went to Xerxes. He gave a full explanation of what he had seen in his dream and then spoke as follows. 'My lord, being human I have already seen **many great states fall at the hands of the less powerful**. I didn't want to allow you to yield entirely to your youthful spirit. I know that it is a bad thing always to want for more; I remember what happened to Cyrus' expedition against the **Massagetae**. I remember what happened to Cambyses' expedition against the **Ethiopians**, and I accompanied Darius on his campaign against the **Scythians**. Knowing all this, I was of the opinion that you would be the most fortunate of all men if you led a life of peace. But since your ambition is something divine and, as it seems, **the destruction that is coming to the Greeks is god-driven**, I myself now turn about and change my mind. Now tell the Persians of the messages that have come from god. Order them to follow the first orders that you gave about preparations. Since god is granting you this, do everything you can to ensure that there is no failure in your own preparations.' 280 285 290

These were the words of Artabanus and they [Xerxes and Artabanus] were so elated by the vision that, as soon as it was day, Xerxes told the Persians everything and from that point Artabanus, who had been the sole voice of opposition before, was a clear enthusiast for the enterprise. 295

---

to turn aside the inevitable   the dream speaks like Apollo's account of the fate of Croesus (1.91, pp. 19–20). It is fated that the expedition will happen and that it will be a disaster.

many great states fall at the hands of the less powerful   Artabanus' words recall Herodotus' own at the beginning of his work, where he talks of the small becoming great and vice versa (1.5, p. 7).

Massagetae   see the note on 7.8 (p. 51) for Cyrus' attack on and defeat by the Massagetae.

Ethiopians   Cambyses' campaign against the Ethiopians was a disaster (3.25).

Scythians   see the note on 7.10a for Darius' unsuccessful campaign against the Scythians.

the destruction that is coming to the Greeks is god-driven   Artabanus is wrong: the destruction that is coming to the *Persians* is god-driven. Like Croesus with his oracle from Delphi about destroying a great empire (1.91, p. 20), he misunderstands the message.

---

1 What are Xerxes' motives for invasion? How coherent are they?

2 What are the different reasons for invasion brought before Xerxes?

3 What are Mardonius and Artabanus like? How effective is Herodotus' characterization of them?

4 How good a mechanism for decision-making is the Persian court?

5 What are we to make of the intervention of the dream? What did the Greeks think of dreams? What have other ages thought of dreams?

6 This debate shows the difficulty of decision-making. Consider other historical or contemporary events in which such difficulties have been significant.

Xerxes and Pythius 1: 7.27–9

Once the decision had been made, three years were spent in making the necessary preparations across the empire. Finally, in spring 480 BC, the expedition set out from Persia and travelled through Lydia towards the coast of Ionia. In Lydia Xerxes met Pythius, a Lydian of immense wealth.

7.27   In the city of **Celaenae, Pythius, the son of Atys,** a Lydian, was waiting for Xerxes. He provided hospitality for the whole of the king's army – a massive undertaking – and for the king himself. He also offered money, wishing to lend his support to the war. In response to Pythius' offer, Xerxes asked the Persians there who Pythius was and how much money he had to make such an offer. 'My 5 lord,' they said, 'this is the man who gave your father, Darius, the golden plane tree and the golden vine. Of all the people we know, he is now **the first in wealth after you.**'

Celaenae   today this is the town of Dinar, which is 125 miles inland from the Ionian coast of the Aegean (see map on p. 9).

Pythius, the son of Atys   Croesus' son was called Atys: for his inadvertent killing see 1.34–45. The name may make us think back to Croesus and his meeting with Solon. Indeed, Pythius may be the son of the Atys of that story and so the grandson of Croesus. That would explain his wealth. Pythius' name would also suggest a link with Delphi: Apollo is worshipped at Delphi as 'Pythian Apollo' (see the image of the Temple of Apollo on p. 100), his priestess is the 'Pythian priestess' and the games held there were the Pythian games.

the first in wealth after you   once again this reminds us of Croesus, his wealth and his confidence in his wealth (1.30, pp. 10–11). Perhaps this should make us wary about Pythius' fate.

7.28 Xerxes **was amazed** to hear the last part of what they said, so then he asked Pythius directly how much **money** he had. 'My lord,' replied Pythius, 'I won't deceive you or pretend that I don't know the size of my fortune. I know what it is and I'll tell you exactly. As soon as I heard that you were coming to the Greek sea, I wanted to make a contribution to the war so I made a thorough **enquiry** into my wealth and I **discovered** through my **calculations** that I have 2,000 **talents** of silver and I'm just 7,000 short of having 4,000,000 **daric staters**. I am going to give all of this to you, since I have **enough to live on** from my slaves and farm-workers.' 10

15

7.29 Xerxes was delighted at his reply and said: 'My Lydian friend, since I left the land of Persia, I have come across no one apart from you who has been willing to offer hospitality to my army, and no one apart from you who, by his own choice, has come to me to contribute funds towards the war. But you have offered hospitality on a grand scale to my army and you are now offering me great sums of money. In return for all this, I will now give you this reward. I will make you my **guest-friend** and from my own resources I will give you the 7,000 staters to make up the figure of 4,000,000 staters, so that you aren't 7,000 staters short of 4,000,000 staters. In this way I will ensure that you have a nice round number. Keep what you have and make sure that you don't change. Never, now or in the future, will you regret what you have done.' 20

25

---

was amazed a key theme of Herodotus' narrative of the invasion is the varied, and unpredictable, responses of Xerxes to events. It is never clear how he is going to react. It is worth tracing that in these chapters and beyond (see 7.29 (above), 7.39 (p. 67), 7.44 (p. 69) and throughout the narrative of Thermopylae and Salamis).

money, enquiry, discovered, calculations Pythius uses the same language as Solon in his discussion with Croesus (1.32, pp. 13–14). However, Pythius is good at counting money, whereas Solon was good at counting the days of life. In the next chapter, Xerxes joins in by completing the calculation. On the other hand, Pythius knows how much he has got, whereas Xerxes has so much that he doesn't even know how much.

talents a talent is 26 kilograms of silver and is worth 6,000 drachmas. A drachma was, in fifth-century Athens, a day's pay for a skilled workman, as we learn from the accounts of the building of the Parthenon.

daric staters named after Darius, the daric stater was the coinage of the Persian empire. It weighed 130 grams and was made of silver. Pythius' pile of money would suggest that there were plenty of darics in circulation. Dwelling on the fault line between Greece and Persia, he has money from both of these worlds.

enough to live on this recalls Solon's account of Tellos' happiness (1.30, p. 11). However, Pythius' 'enough to live on' from his slaves and farm-workers is likely to be rather different from Tellos'.

guest-friend one of the key ties that bound Greek society together was the concept of guest-friendship, the reciprocal arrangement where the giving and accepting of hospitality created a long-term relationship. In ancient Greek the word *xenos* means stranger, guest, host and friend. For one of the earliest examples of this in Greek literature, compare the meeting of Glaucus and Diomedes in the *Iliad* 6.120–238. See also guest-friendship in operation in 9.76 (pp. 138–9) between Pausanias and a woman from Cos.

The bridge at Abydos: 7.33–6

In order to make the expedition possible, there had to be massive engineering works. A canal was dug across the peninsula of Mount Athos in northern Greece and the Hellespont had to be bridged by means of a pontoon.

7.33   Xerxes now made preparations to advance to **Abydos**. During this period his men had built a bridge across the Hellespont from Asia to Europe. On the Hellespontine Chersonese, between Sestos and Madytus, there is a rough promontory that juts out into the sea opposite Abydos. It was there, not long after this, that the Athenians, under the command of **Xanthippus**, the son of Ariphron, captured 5
Artayctes, the Persian governor of Sestos, and nailed him alive to a plank. For he used to bring women to the shrine of **Protesilaus** in Elaeus and commit dreadful acts of sacrilege.

7.34   Setting out from Abydos to this promontory those responsible for the building of bridges started their task. The Phoenicians built their bridge out of flax 10
and the Egyptians of papyrus. It is seven stades from Abydos to the other side. When the strait had been bridged, a great storm arose, smashing and destroying everything.

7.35   When Xerxes heard this, he took it very badly and gave the command that the Hellespont should receive **300 lashes** and that a pair of fetters should be cast 15
into the sea. I have also heard that he sent some men at the same time to **brand** the Hellespont. And he told those who were doing the flogging to say words of

---

Abydos   the town on the eastern side of the Dardanelles. At its narrowest the strait is 1 mile wide (see map on p. 9).

Xanthippus, Artayctes, Protesilaus   Herodotus breaks the chronological process to look forward to the very end of the work and the war (see 9.116–22, pp. 142–6). It serves as a reminder of where Xerxes' grand design will end. Xanthippus was an Athenian general, but his historic greatness really lies in being the father of Pericles, the greatest leader of the Athenian democracy in the fifth century BC. Protesilaus was the first Greek to leap ashore at the beginning of the Trojan War, and the first Greek to die. This echo takes us back to the earliest part of Herodotus' narrative, the events from early history that mark the historical enmity between East and West (1.3, pp. 5–6).

300 lashes, brand   this is Xerxes' usual way of dealing with insubordination or failure, as he shows at Thermopylae (see 7.223, p. 93). He is not the first Persian king to get angry with nature: Cyrus does the same to the river Gyndes (1.189–90). Darius, on the other hand, shows rather more respect to the Bosporus and to the man who built the bridge over it (see 4.85, 87–8, 91).

barbarity and folly: 'You bitter waters, your master imposes this **punishment** on you because you have done him **wrong**, although he has done you no wrong. **Xerxes, the king of Persia, will cross over**, whether you want it or not. It is only right that no man should sacrifice to you; you're just a dirty salt river.' This was the punishment that he commanded for the sea, but, as for those who were in charge of the bridging of the Hellespont, he gave the command that they should be beheaded.

7.36 The appointed men performed this thankless task and different architects completed the bridge.

> The bridge was finally constructed so that the army could cross. According to Herodotus, the bridge involved binding together 674 ships to form the pontoon (7.36).

Xerxes and Pythius 2: 7.37–40

7.37 The army wintered at Sardis and, having made its preparations, departed at the beginning of spring and set out for Abydos. When they had set out, **the sun left its place in the heavens** and disappeared, even though there were no clouds and the sky was absolutely clear. Night replaced day. When Xerxes realized what he had seen he was troubled. So he asked the **magi** what the sight was meant to signify. Their reply was that god was showing to the Greeks the eclipse of their cities: they argued that the sun gave signs to the Greeks, whereas the moon gave signs to the Persians. Xerxes was delighted at this answer and he continued the advance.

---

barbarity and folly, punishment, wrong   Xerxes' words and actions are troubling. This is not the way for a human being to behave or to be successful. Getting cross with Pythius and his advisers, as he is about to do, is one thing, but such treatment of the natural world and disrespect for the divine is an act of moral outrage that runs the risk of divine punishment. Herodotus also conveys elsewhere that there is something unnatural and therefore ominous about changing nature: the people of Cnidos are warned against cutting through an isthmus to make themselves into an island (1.174).

Xerxes, the king of Persia, will cross over   Xerxes slips into the third person: compare Shakespeare's *Julius Caesar* (Act 2, Scene 2, line 48): 'And Caesar shall go forth.'

the sun left its place in the heavens   for the importance of such an event, compare the eclipse that ended the battle between the Lydians and Medians (1.74). There is no eclipse that occurred at the right time for this event, but one did occur in Susa on 18 April 481 BC. Perhaps this was transposed to this moment.

magi   Herodotus (1.107) says that the magi are a distinct Median tribe, but he is alone in doing this. Elsewhere in Herodotus, they are an essential presence at Persian sacrifices (1.132) and they are the interpreters of dreams for the Persian kings (1.107, 7.19). One of them also plays a critical part in the downfall of Cambyses and the selection of Darius as king (3.61–80).

7.38 When Xerxes was continuing his advance, Pythius the Lydian, terrified by the sight from heaven and encouraged by Xerxes' gifts, came to see him and said, 'Master, there is something that I need from you. It is a small thing for you to help me in, but it's important to me.'

Xerxes, who thought that his request would be anything other than what it actually was, said that he would help and told him to say what he wanted. On hearing this, Pythius was encouraged and said, 'Master, I have five sons, and it happens that all five of them are with you on this expedition to Greece. My lord, take pity on me, old as I am, and excuse my oldest son from this campaign, so that he might be the guardian of me and my fortune. Take the other four with you and I pray that you will return home with your purpose fulfilled.'

7.39 Xerxes was incandescent with rage. 'You scum!' he replied. 'How dare you mention your son when I am making an invasion of Greece with my sons and brothers and household and friends? You are my slave and you should be following me with all of your household, including your wife. Now, understand this. **A man's spirit dwells in his ears.** When he hears good things, his body fills with delight. When he hears the opposite, it swells up with anger. When you did me a favour and undertook to do more, you could not boast that you excelled the king in generosity. But now you have turned to shamelessness and you will not get your deserts. You will get less than you deserve. Your acts of hospitality protect you and your four sons, but you will pay with the life of the one son whom you were most bothered about.'

This was Xerxes' reply and then he ordered those who had been made responsible for such tasks to find the oldest of Pythius' sons and **cut him in half**, and, when they had done so, to put half of his body on the right-hand side of the road and the other half on the left.

7.40 And so they did this and the army marched through the middle.

A man's spirit dwells in his ears   this is an odd way of talking, but it is certainly true of the way in which Xerxes acts.

cut him in half   Pythius' son is not the last person to be cut up on Xerxes' orders: some Phoenicians, the best sailors in the Persian fleet at Salamis, were decapitated (8.90, p. 113). Darius had been equally fierce to Oeobazus, a man who made a similar request for his sons in the invasion of Scythia (4.84). Some scholars argue that this sacrifice is a form of purification of the army as it sets out on its invasion.

1 What impression do we gain of Xerxes from these passages?

2 What do the stories tell us about the nature of the Persians and the expedition?

3 How significant is the supernatural in these passages?

4 Does the narrative create a sense of future disaster? If so, how?

5 Where could Herodotus have got his evidence for all of this?

6 Why does Herodotus' narrative have so much dialogue?

7 In what ways does the meeting of Xerxes and Pythius remind us of the meeting of Solon and Croesus? Why would Herodotus want to emphasize those similarities?

Xerxes and Artabanus at Abydos: 7.43–53

7.43 And so the army came to the river **Scamander**. This was the first river they had come across that failed them since setting out from Sardis on their journey; it was drunk dry by the army and its animals. When Xerxes came to the river, he was possessed by the desire to go up and see **Pergamon, the citadel of Priam**. When he had seen and learnt about all the details, **he sacrificed a thousand bulls to Athena, and the magi poured libations to the heroes**. When they had done this, **fear** fell upon the army that night. At daybreak, he set out from there. 5

Scamander, Pergamon, the citadel of Priam Scamander is one of two rivers that flow through the plain of Troy: the Trojan hero Hector calls his son Scamandrios (Homer *Iliad* 6.400). Pergamon is one of the names given to the city of Troy. The inclusion of this story places Xerxes' invasion in the context both of the historic confrontations between East and West (see 1.1–5, pp. 3–7) and of the world of heroic deeds.

he sacrificed a thousand bulls to Athena, and the magi poured libations to the heroes it is interesting that Xerxes here performs Greek religious observances, sacrificing to Athena and pouring libations to the cult heroes of Homer's narrative. The Greeks believed that the great heroes continued to have force after their deaths, so that they poured libations to them in the places they were buried. For heroes active in events, see the significance of the bones of Orestes (1.67–8) to the Spartans, or the sons of Aeacus summoned from Aegina before the battle of Salamis (8.64, p. 102). See also 5.80–1 and the entry in the *Oxford Classical Dictionary* on hero-cult.

fear presumably the Persians are struck by fear because of their recollection of the fate of the Trojans at the hands of the Greeks.

7.44 When they were at **Abydos,** Xerxes wanted to see the whole of his army. **A throne of white stone** had already been made for him on a hill for this very purpose – the people of Abydos had made it for him on his orders. As he sat there, with 10 a view over the shore, he looked upon the land army and the ships, and, as he looked, he was struck by a desire to watch a **ship race**. And so it happened and the **Phoenicians from Sidon won the race**. Xerxes was **delighted** both by the race and by his forces.

7.45 When he saw the whole of the Hellespont hidden by ships, and all the promontories 15 and plains of Abydos full of men, Xerxes declared himself the **most fortunate** of men. **Then he burst into tears.**

7.46 Artabanus, his uncle, noticed this. He had been **the first person to speak freely** to Xerxes, advising him not to invade Greece. And when this man realized that Xerxes was crying, he said to him, 'My lord, you are now doing the exact opposite 20 of what you did just before. Then you thought yourself fortunate. Now, you are in tears.' 'I was thinking,' said Xerxes, 'and it came in to my mind to feel pity at the **brevity of all human life**. Of all the vast number of people gathered here,

---

Abydos   the town nearest to the Hellespont, the narrowest crossing from Asia to Europe. It is also the scene of a famous myth, that of Hero and Leander. Hero was a priestess of Aphrodite at Sestus whilst Leander lived in Abydos. He used to swim to see his beloved until the light by which he was guided was blown out in a storm and he was drowned. Hero threw herself to her death in grief.

A throne of white stone   Xerxes watches the engagements at Thermopylae (7.212, p. 88) and Salamis from a throne set up for the purpose (8.90, p. 113). For Xerxes war is a spectator sport, but the Greek generals are participants.

ship race   the idea of races recalls the epic athletic contests held at the Funeral Games of Patroclus in Homer's *Iliad*, Book 23. As ever, Xerxes is concerned with appearances and display, whilst his wise adviser Artabanus is concerned with reality.

Phoenicians from Sidon won the race   the Phoenicians were the finest sailors in the Persian force. It is ironic, and indicative of Xerxes' nature, that after the battle of Salamis they are unjustly beheaded by Xerxes for their failure in the battle (8.90, p. 113). Even on his way home Xerxes rewards and then beheads a Phoenician sea-captain (8.118).

delighted, most fortunate, Then he burst into tears   once again we see the unpredictability of Xerxes. The scene is also intended to echo the meeting of Solon and Croesus: Xerxes is like Croesus in believing that the scale of his prosperity renders him fortunate, but Artabanus' wisdom about the nature of human life recalls Solon's philosophy. Both Herodotus' history and Greek tragedy are full of the theme of the 'tragic warner', the man who can see the future, but is ignored. For example, Tiresias, the blind seer in Sophocles' *Antigone*, knows what is right but at first is ignored.

the first person to speak freely   a reference to the debate about the invasion (7.10, p. 55). It does Artabanus little good to tell the truth now or then.

brevity of all human life   Xerxes is concerned about the brevity of human life whereas Solon (1.32, p. 14) and Artabanus are more worried by its mutability.

not one of them will be alive in a hundred years.' And Artabanus replied, 'It is our fate to suffer something even more pitiable than this in our lives. For even in 25 so short a life, there is no man, either amongst these men or anywhere else, who is so fortunate that it will not occur to him, not once, but often, that **he would rather be dead than alive.** For misfortunes fall upon us, diseases confound us and they make a short life seem long. And so, since our life is so wearisome, death is the most desirable of refuges for a man, and god, who gives us a taste of life's 30 sweetness, turns out to be grudging in this gift.'

7.47   'Artabanus,' replied Xerxes. 'Human life is as you describe it, **but let's talk no more about it.** Let's not dwell on our troubles when we have good fortune in our grasp. Now, tell me this. If that vision in your dream had not appeared to you so clearly, would you have stood by your original opinion and not allowed me to invade 35 Greece? Or would you have changed your mind? **Come on, tell me straight.**' And Artabanus replied, 'My lord, I wish that the vision in the dream may come to pass as we both wish. And yet, I am still full of fear. Indeed I'm out of my mind with it. I have many concerns, but the biggest is **that the two greatest elements we face are both enemies to us.**'
40

7.48   'My good sir, what two things can you mean that are hostile to us?' replied Xerxes. 'What about our land army? **Isn't it big enough?** Will the Greek army be equal to it? Or will our fleet be inferior to theirs? Or perhaps both things are true. If you think that our forces aren't big enough, someone should go and get another army with all speed.'
45

7.49   Artabanus replied, 'No one of intelligence could find fault with this army or the size of your fleet. If you get more, the two elements of which I speak will be even more of an enemy. These two elements are the land and the sea. For, **by my calculations**, there isn't a harbour anywhere that is big enough to take in your

---

he would rather be dead than alive   Artabanus not only recalls Solon's words (1.32, p. 14). He also echoes something deep in the Greeks' concept of the world, that life isn't really that desirable: 'not to be born is best', sing the chorus in Sophocles' *Oedipus the King*.

but let's talk no more about it   Xerxes, like Croesus, isn't receptive to too much philosophy or advice in general. Therein lies the danger for him.

Come on, tell me straight   Artabanus wisely doesn't give an answer about the dream, but changes the subject and tries to offer some strategic advice.

that the two greatest elements we face are both enemies to us   Artabanus even sounds like the Delphic oracle in that his answer is both enigmatic and paradoxical.

Isn't it big enough?   Xerxes can only think in terms of numbers, and they are big numbers (see 7.184–5, p. 81). The confined spaces of Artemisium, Thermopylae and Salamis will show that he is wrong and Artabanus is right.

by my calculations   Artabanus uses the same language as Solon (1.32, p.13). This time, however, his calculation is a logistical one, based on the nature of Greece and its coastline.

fleet when a storm comes and guarantee the safety of your ships. And yet, you are 50
not going to need one harbour, but a harbour at every place on the coast along
which you are travelling. Since there are no harbours of sufficient size, you must
understand that **events** are the master of men, not men the master of events.
That's one of the two factors. I will now talk about the second. The land is our
enemy in the following way. If nothing stands and opposes you, the further you 55
advance the more of an enemy the land will become. **It will forever be tricking
you onwards. Man is never satisfied with success.** As you meet no resistance, so
I say that the land will bring forth famine that will increase as time goes by. This
is the best way for a man to be. He should be **fearful in his planning, calculating
everything that might go wrong, but in action he should be bold.**' 60

7.50 'Artabanus,' replied Xerxes. 'It's perfectly reasonable for you to make calculations
about every detail, but don't be afraid of everything or give equal weight to
everything. If in every single matter you face you give equal weight to everything,
then you'd never get anything done. It's better to be optimistic in all things and
suffer danger half the time than, being fearful about everything, never suffer 65
anything at all. If you argue over everything that is said, but then don't offer any
sure alternative, you're likely to be proved wrong and turn out no better than the
man who says the opposite. Your argument is no better than his. **Since we are
but men, how can we know anything for sure? I think it's impossible.** As a rule,
success comes to those who are willing to act, not to those who calculate every 70
detail and then hesitate.

---

events   'Man is all chance,' said Solon (1.32, p. 13) and Artabanus repeats the message.
It is a message that has lived on in modern politics. Harold Macmillan, the British Prime
Minister between 1957 and 1963, when asked by a journalist about what worried him
most as Prime Minister, famously said, 'Events, dear boy, events.' He read Classics at
Oxford, so he would have known Herodotus. Donald Rumsfeld, the American Secretary
for Defense between 1975 and 1977 and between 2001 and 2006, expressed a similar
sentiment: 'Stuff happens.'

It will forever be tricking you onwards. Man is never satisfied with success   the Persians
had faced a similar difficulty in their expansion into Scythia (4.126–35). Artabanus'
analysis of nature is very simply presented, but it is an analysis of war that rings through
history. The invasions of Russia by Napoleon and Hitler are examples of the problem of
large-scale invasions of large areas.

fearful … calculating … bold   Artabanus' analysis presents the paradox of leadership in
war: it requires reason, calculation, but also, in the end, the willingness to take risks.

Since we are but men, how can we know anything for sure? I think it's impossible   Xerxes'
response seems quite reasonable, but his response to the uncertainty of human existence
leads him to an entirely opposite conclusion from that of Artabanus: since there is always
uncertainty in life, that should encourage us to take risks.

'Look at the state of Persia, how far we have advanced in power. If **the kings before me** had followed your way of thinking, or, even if they didn't think like that, had advisers like you, you would never have seen us come so far. They took risks and so have brought us to where we are now. **Great things are achieved by the taking** 75 **of great risks**. And so, matching up to those men, we are making our expedition at the best season of the year. We shall subdue all of Europe and will come home again. We won't meet famine anywhere nor suffer anything else untoward. Firstly, we are making our expedition with abundant supplies. Secondly, we can get food from any land or tribe that we come upon. **We are attacking farmers, not** 80 **nomads.**'

7.51 After this Artabanus said, 'My lord, even though you won't allow me to worry about anything, at least accept my advice. For matters of great moment require greater consideration. **Cyrus, the son of Cambyses, conquered all of Ionia except Athens** and made it pay tribute to the Persians. **My advice to you**, therefore, is that 85 you should certainly not lead the Ionians against their fathers. We can gain the upper hand over our enemies without them. If they follow us they must commit an act of the greatest injustice in enslaving their **mother city**. If they act justly, they will join in securing its freedom. If they do the former, they won't be much good to us. If the latter, they are capable of doing great harm to your campaign. 90 You should ponder in your heart the wise old saying, "**The end isn't visible at the beginning.**"'

---

the kings before me, Great things are achieved by the taking of great risks Xerxes returns to the need to emulate his predecessors (see 7.8, pp. 51–2) even though his predecessors were not uniformly successful. Once again the language echoes the Bisitun inscription (see pp. 76–7). As it turns out, Artabanus' analysis does seem overpessimistic in that there isn't much in Herodotus about the problems of supply. Other factors do turn out to be more important in the account. However, once again Artabanus is raising one of the key issues of warfare throughout the ages, the issue of logistics.

We are attacking farmers, not nomads Darius' invasion of Scythia was made very difficult because he was trying to conquer nomads (see Coes' advice (4.97)).

Cyrus, the son of Cambyses, conquered all of Ionia except Athens this conquest (1.156–77) came as the consequence of the Ionian revolt (499–494 BC). The Persians see Athens and the cities of Ionia as being one group because, originally, Athens is a city populated by Ionians, not Dorians, and the cities of Ionia looked back to Athens as their original home.

My advice to you Artabanus has failed on the big issue, so he turns to a specific piece of advice about the Ionians. As it turns out, the Ionians do not do much harm to the Persian invasion, despite Themistocles' attempt to win them over by leaving messages encouraging them to defect (8.22, and 8.85 on p.111).

mother city Athens

The end isn't visible at the beginning compare, once again, Solon's advice to Croesus to look to the end of everything (1.32, p.14).

7.52 'Artabanus,' Xerxes replied, 'of all the advice you have offered, this is where you are most mistaken. You are wrong to worry that the Ionians will change sides. We have the strongest proof of this, and you were a witness of it, and so were **all those** **who went on campaign against Scythia with Darius.** The destruction or survival of the whole Persian expedition was in their hands. They acted with justice and loyalty and did nothing wrong. Anyway, they have left their children and wives and possessions in our country, so they can't even consider causing any trouble. So, don't worry about this, but be confident and look after my household and my kingdom. I am entrusting to you alone my power.' 95 100

7.53 Having said this, **Xerxes sent Artabanus back to Susa** and summoned, for the second time, the most distinguished Persians. When they were all present, he spoke to them as follows. 'Persians, I have brought you all here to require of you that you should show your courage and not disgrace the mighty and glorious deeds performed by the Persians in the past. We must all, each one of us, be fully committed to the task. For it is the shared purpose that spurs us on. I urge you to prosecute this war vigorously for the following reason. As I hear, we are going to war against men of courage. If we beat them, there will be no other force that will ever stand to face us. But now, let us pray to the gods who hold the land of Persia and cross over the bridge.' 105 110

> 1 What issues does Artabanus raise in this debate?
>
> 2 How good an answer does Xerxes give to Artabanus' concerns?
>
> 3 What does this dialogue contribute to the narrative?
>
> 4 What are the parallels with the meeting between Solon and Croesus? What do the parallels tell us?
>
> 5 How real are the issues of leadership, risk, danger and empire here? Consider other examples in history of the risks of great invasions and the final outcome.

all those who went on campaign against Scythia with Darius   see note on Histiaeus at 7.10c. Although the Ionians stood firm in support of Darius then, later they did revolt against the Persian empire in the Ionian revolt (499–494 BC), led by some of the Ionian tyrants who were at the bridge over the Danube.

Xerxes sent Artabanus back to Susa   so Xerxes very simply gets rid of his key adviser, just as Croesus let Solon go.

Xerxes and Demaratus at Doriscus: 7.100–5

After crossing the Hellespont from Abydos, Xerxes' army advanced through Thrace to Doriscus, a site by the river Hebrus where the Persians had kept a garrison from the time of Darius. Here Xerxes held a review of his troops and Herodotus uses this moment to give his account of the Persian forces (7.60–99) and to have another dialogue of warning. That account tells in remarkable detail the nature of all the different nationalities. In so doing, it gives an epic scale to the story and recalls Homer's *Iliad* 2, in which the Greek forces at Troy are listed.

7.100 **When the army had been counted** and drawn up, Xerxes wanted to ride through the army and inspect it, so that's what he did. Riding in his chariot amongst all the different races he asked about each one and **the scribes recorded it all**, until he had travelled from one end to the other, seeing the infantry and the cavalry. When this was done, the ships were dragged down to the sea and then Xerxes transferred 5 from his chariot to a ship from **Sidon**. He sat under a golden canopy and he sailed along the prows of the ships. He made enquiries of each of them, just as he had done with the land forces and it was all written down. The ships' captains put out to sea to a distance of about four **plethra** from the shore and there they rode at anchor, turning their prows to the land, all in a line. The marines were armed as 10 for battle. Xerxes made his inspection sailing between the ships and the shore.

7.101 When Xerxes had carried out his inspection, he disembarked and sent for **Demaratus, the son of Ariston**, who was with him on the campaign against Greece. He called him and asked, 'Demaratus, I'd really like to ask you about something I want to know. You are a Greek and, as I understand from you and the other Greeks with 15 whom I talk, you are from a city that is not the least or the weakest. Now, tell me

---

When the army had been counted although Herodotus has given his account of the Persian forces in the previous chapters, he saves the final calculation for Thermopylae, where they first face the Greeks in earnest (7.184–5, p. 81).

the scribes recorded it all this is typical of the Persian approach, as surviving inscriptions show. Presumably, Herodotus used such a source for his account. At the battle of Salamis, Xerxes ensures that the greatest achievements in the battle are similarly preserved (8.90, p. 113). Could this have been a source for Herodotus?

Sidon one of the two major cities of Phoenicia.

plethra a plethron is 100 feet, 29.6 metres.

Demaratus, the son of Ariston under the Spartan constitution there were two kings from two royal families. Demaratus was deposed in 491 BC in a dispute about his legitimacy and fled to Persia, where he was taken in by Darius (6.62–70). Demaratus even has a voice in the choice of Xerxes as Darius' heir (7.3). He is one of the key interlocutors with Xerxes not only here, but at Thermopylae (7.209, p. 86).

this. Will the Greeks stand their ground and fight me? In my opinion, not even if all the Greeks and everyone else who dwells to the west were to gather together, would they be capable of resisting my attack. There aren't enough of them. However, I want to find this out from you. What have you to say about this?' 20

That was his question and Demaratus replied, 'My lord, **do you want me to tell you the truth or say what you want to hear?**' Xerxes told him to tell the truth and said that this would do him no harm.

7.102   On hearing this, Demaratus spoke. 'My lord, you order me to tell you only the truth, so that I won't be caught as a liar in the future. Well, the Greeks have always 25 been brought up with **poverty, but courage they have got for themselves, achieved through wisdom and the strength of the law. In this way, they keep poverty and despotism at bay.** I have high regard for all the Greeks who inhabit the **Dorian territories.** However, what I am about to say does not apply to all of them, but only to the Spartans. First of all, they will never listen to your words that bring slavery 30 to Greece. Secondly, they will stand and face you in battle, even if all the other Greeks come over to you. Don't ask about their numbers or how many men they have got to be able to do such a thing. If they've got 1,000 men out on campaign, they will fight you with them. And they'll fight with less or with more.'

7.103   When he heard this, **Xerxes laughed.** 'Demaratus, what a thing to say! Will a 35 thousand men really fight against an army this size? Come on, tell me. You say that you were once a king of these people. Would you really be willing to fight ten men? And yet, if your constitution is entirely as you describe, you should, as their king, stand against twice that number according to your own laws. If each of the Spartans is worth ten men in my army, I insist that you are worth twenty. 40

---

do you want me to tell you the truth or say what you want to hear?   Demaratus, as a king himself, knows the problems of dealing with a king, both for the king and for the subject. At least he gets a guarantee that he is safe. Perhaps it is easier for a foreign king to tell Xerxes the truth than for his own subjects to do so.

poverty … courage … wisdom … the strength of the law … despotism at bay   Demaratus here identifies the qualities that, according to the Greeks themselves, won them this war. Although Demaratus at this point claims to be talking about all the Greeks, these words apply particularly to the Spartans. They prided themselves on creating a unique way of life dedicated to military prowess and obedience that saved them from tyranny and made them the most feared people in Greece. Demaratus' realism contrasts with Mardonius' account of Greece as a green and pleasant land (7.5, p. 50).

Dorian territories   as explained previously, mainland Greece was largely occupied by Dorian Greeks, whereas the Athenians were Ionians. Demaratus shows that Spartans think that, in the end, only the Spartans are truly great warriors, but the war proves that this is not entirely so.

Xerxes laughed   Xerxes laughs twice at Demaratus in this dialogue, here and in 7.105, p. 78.

Bisitun inscription

From the beginning of Herodotus' account of the invasion of 480 BC, Xerxes is presented as being very conscious of not falling short of his predecessors or their high level of energetic conquest. This attitude is matched in the Bisitun inscription, carved in three languages onto the cliff face of Mount Bisitun in north-west Iran, on the Royal Road which ran from Babylon to Ecbatana. It is Darius' account of his reign and was completed *c.* 520 BC.

I am Darius, the Great King, king of kings, king of Persia, king of lands, the son of Hytaspes, the grandson of Arsames, and Achaemenid.

*Darius the king says: 'There are eight in my family who formerly have been kings. I am the ninth king. Thus we are **nine kings in succession**.'*

*Darius the king says: 'These are the countries which belong to me. By the favour of **Ahura Mazda** I was their king: **Persia, Elam, Babylonia, Assyria**, Arabia, Egypt, the People by the Sea, Lydia, Ionia, Media, Armenia, Cappadocia, Parthia, Drangiana, Aria, Chorasmia, Bactria, Sogdiana, Gandara, Scythia, Sattagydia, Arachosia and Maka, altogether twenty-three countries.'*

nine kings in succession scholars can't come to an agreement about his eight predecessors. Darius was not actually a member of the royal house.

Ahura Mazda the great god of the Persian kings whose name is attested from Darius on. He was the creator of the world and following Ahura Mazda involved following the right path and rejecting the Lie.

Persia, Elam, Babylonia, Assyria the list starts with the four central territories of the Persian empire and then goes in a clockwise direction.

Darius the king says: 'In these countries, the man who was loyal, I treated well, who was disloyal, I punished severely. By the favour of Ahura Mazda, these countries obeyed my law. As I said to them, thus they used to do.'

Darius the king says: 'By the favour of Ahura Mazda also I have done much more that has not been written down in this inscription; for this reason it has not been written down, lest what I have done should seem too much to him who will read this inscription hereafter, and this should not convince him, but he regard it as false.'

Darius the king says: 'In their entire lives, previous kings have not done so much as I, by the favour of Ahura Mazda, have done in one and the same year.'

LACTOR 16: *The Persian Empire from Cyrus II to Artaxerxes I*, translated and edited with notes by Maria Brosius.

1 How does the Bisitun inscription compare with Herodotus' picture of the Persian king?

2 What is the purpose of such an inscription? How valuable is it as a source? How does it differ from a historical narrative? Compare 3.89–97 for Herodotus' account of the structure of the Persian empire.

In that case you would prove what you've said. If, however, they are of the same type and size as you and the other Greeks who have come to see me, in that case you are just showing off. You'd better be careful that these words of yours don't turn out to be just an empty boast. Let's take a look at this reasonably. How could 1,000 men or even 10,000 or even 50,000 who were **free and not under the rule** 45 **of one man** stand against an army like this one. If there are 5,000 of them we outnumber them 1,000 to one. They might fight if they were **under the rule of one man, according to our system out of fear of this man.** They might show courage beyond their own natures and go into battle against the odds, **driven on by the lash.** But if they are entirely free, they would not do any of this. Indeed, it 50 is my opinion that, even if the Greeks had equal numbers, they would find it hard to fight only the Persians. Our men have the quality of which you speak. It is not common, but it is to be found. Some of the Persian bodyguard would be willing to fight three Greeks simultaneously. But you don't know anything about this and you're talking total nonsense.' 55

7.104 To this Demaratus replied, 'My lord, I knew right from the start that, if I told you the truth, I'd say things that you didn't like. You forced me to tell the whole truth,

---

free and not under the rule of one man, under the rule of one man, according to our system out of fear of this man, driven on by the lash Xerxes doesn't understand any way of life other than autocracy, fear and the lash. This dialogue brings out the fact that this is a war where two ideological worlds meet.

so I told you what is required of the **Spartiates**. You know only too well what my feelings are now about these people who have robbed me of my ancestral honour and rights and made me an exile without a city. Your father took me in and gave me a livelihood and a place to live. A man of good sense should not spurn goodwill when it is offered. He should welcome it gladly. I admit that I couldn't fight ten men, or even two men. In fact, I don't even want to fight one-on-one. But if I must, or there is some great cause to spur me on, I would gladly fight one of those men who says that he is the equal of three Greeks. Fighting man for man, the Spartans are no worse than anyone else, but together they are the best of all. **For they are free, but not entirely free. For law is their master.** They fear it much more than your subjects fear you. They do whatever it commands, and it always commands the same thing. **It does not allow them to flee battle, whatever the odds.** They must stay in their battle line and win or die. If you think that in saying so I am talking nonsense, I'll say no more in the future. But you forced me to speak, so I did. I hope that things turn out as you would want, my lord.'

7.105   This was Demaratus' reply, but Xerxes just laughed. He showed no anger but sent him away with all good humour.

---

1   What does Demaratus bring to the dialogue with Xerxes?
2   What are the key issues about the war that the dialogue introduces?
3   Why do you think that Herodotus presents his analysis in this dialogic form?
4   How did the 'Spartan myth' develop in Greece?

Spartiates   the Spartiates were the warrior elite of the Spartan nation whose entire life and upbringing was dedicated to military prowess. They were a small and dwindling proportion of the population of Sparta.

For they are free, but not entirely free. For law is their master   this is the simplest and most important Greek response to the Persian way of being and an answer to the question of why the Greeks beat such an overwhelming force.

It does not allow them to flee battle, whatever the odds   Demaratus foresees the myth of Thermopylae and the 300 Spartans. In the Second World War much of Churchill's rhetoric was similar: 'we will never surrender' and the insistence on the triumph of 'the few' in the battle of Britain.

6 The battle of Thermopylae, 480 BC

The Persian invasion, 480 BC.

The Greeks had no single response to the Persian invasion and there was no reason why they should, being a collection of separate city-states. Many decided to surrender in the face of such overwhelming numbers, and only about 40 states (out of several hundred in the Greek world) actually opposed the Persians. Even these 40 had different ideas about where and how to resist. The most powerful Greek state in military terms at the time was Sparta, and the Spartans were always reluctant to leave the stronghold of their own territory, let alone the Peloponnese. However, others saw the need to resist the Persians in the north and thereby protect city-states north of the Isthmus of Corinth. Therefore, a Greek force of 10,000 men did go to Thessaly (7.173-4). But, on the advice of Alexander, king of Macedon and the ancestor of Alexander the Great, that force retreated once again to the Isthmus for further debate. Only then was it decided to go north to Artemisium, on the northern tip of Euboea, and Thermopylae, the narrow pass close by on the coast.

The resistance against massive odds and the ultimate death of King Leonidas and the 300 Spartans has become, as J. F. Lazenby (see Recommended reading) wrote, 'one of the most famous days in the history of warfare'. The Spartan bravery and obedience to the death is the very foundation of the myth of Sparta. Like Dunkirk or the Alamo, posterity made defeat into a strange act of glory. And yet it was a defeat which exposed all of central Greece to the Persians and resulted in a disastrous loss of Spartan lives.

Thermopylae and Artemisium: 7.175, 177

7.175 When the Greeks came to the Isthmus, they held a debate in the light of Alexander's information as to how and where they should face the enemy. Their decision was that they should defend the pass at Thermopylae; it was narrower than the pass in Thessaly and nearer their own territory. As for the path by means of which the Greeks were trapped at Thermopylae, they knew nothing about it 5 before they reached Thermopylae where the people of Trachis told them about it. The Greek plan was to hold this pass and thereby prevent the barbarians from entering Greece. In addition, their fleet was to sail to **Artemisium**, in the territory of Histiaiotis. The two places are near to each other and this allowed for good communication.

10

Artemisium   the map on p. 79 shows the proximity of Thermopylae and Cape Artemisium. However, it is not only the proximity that makes this a place of strategic significance. If the Greek fleet could hold this position, they would force the Persian fleet to travel down the exposed, east side of Euboea, a notoriously rough and harbourless stretch of sea, and detach it from the land forces.

7.177   These two places [Thermopylae and Artemisium] seemed to be the best to the Greeks. After calculation and consideration of the fact that the barbarians would not be able to use their superiority in numbers or their cavalry, they decided to face their advance into Greece at this point. When they learnt that the Persians were at **Pieria, they broke up their conference** at the Isthmus and set out – the   15
land forces to Thermopylae, the fleet to Artemisium.

The Persian numbers: 7.184–7

7.184   The [Persian] army came to Thermopylae without suffering any difficulties. At this point, according to my enquiries and calculations, the fleet from Asia had 1,207 ships with the original complement of 241,000, on the basis that there were, on average, 200 men on each ship. On each ship there were 30 marines, either Persians or Medes or Sacae, in addition to the native marines. That is an additional   5
36,210 men. I will also add to this number the men from the **penteconters**, 80 men on each, more or less. There were 3,000 of these vessels, as I've said before, so there would be 240,000 men on them. This was the fleet from Asia, in total 517,610. The infantry was a force of 1,700,000 and the cavalry was 800,000. I will also add to this the camel drivers from Egypt and the chariot-drivers from   10
Libya, making a total of 20,000. So the total figure for the land and sea forces put together was 2,317,610. This was the army that came from Asia, not including servants who were in attendance and the provision ships and all the men who sailed with them.

7.185   It is also necessary to add to this total the army which joined from Europe. Whereas   15
the first figure was calculated, this can only be an estimate. The Greeks from Thrace and from the neighbouring islands provided 120 ships. That is a total of 24,000 men from these ships. The **Paionians** and the Eordi and the Bottiaioi and the people of Chalcidice and the Brugoi and the Pierians and the Macedonians and the Perraiboi and the Enienians and the Dolopes and the Magnetes and   20
the Achaeans and all who dwell on the coast of Thrace, provided 30,000 men. When these myriads are added to those from Asia, the total fighting forces are 2,641,610.

Pieria   60 miles north of Thermopylae and no further away from there than the Isthmus of Corinth. Therefore, speed is of the essence for the Greeks to get to Thermopylae from the Isthmus.

they broke up their conference   throughout the Persian invasion the Greeks are usually arguing when something needs to be done. This is most obvious at Salamis. However, this is one incident amongst many that shows the haste and incompleteness of the Greek defence plan.

penteconters   these are oared ships smaller than a trireme, with 50 oarsmen.

Paionians   all these places and peoples are from northern Greece, which Xerxes has already overrun.

7.186 This is the total of the fighting forces, but as for the attendants and those on the provision ships and on the other ships which accompanied the expedition, 25 I would suggest that they were not fewer in number, but more. So, I am going to make them equal in number, not less and not more. If they are equal to the fighting force, then they must match them in numbers. And so Xerxes, the son of Darius, led **5,283,320 men** as far as Sepias and Thermopylae.

7.187 This, then, is the number of the total forces of the army of Xerxes. As for the 30 women, cooks and prostitutes and eunuchs, no one could give a definite figure. As for the yoke-animals and the other beasts of burden and the Indian hounds that accompanied the expedition, the very number makes calculation impossible. And so it is no wonder that some rivers ran dry, but it is a wonder that they had enough supplies for so many myriads. By my calculations I find that, if each soldier had 35 a **choinix** of grain each day and no more, 110,340 **medimnai** would be used up each day. I have not included in my calculation the women or the eunuchs or the yoke-animals or the dogs. But from all of that army of so many myriads, **none was more worthy in beauty or stature to hold this power than Xerxes.**

> When the Persian fleet came to Cape Artemisium, it was badly damaged by a severe storm: according to Herodotus, 400 ships were lost. Thereafter, a number of Persian ships were also captured by the Greek fleet.

5,283,320 men   Herodotus gives his account of the Persian contingents at Doriscus, but he saves his final calculation of the numbers for the moment when the forces first come to the edge of actual engagement. Herodotus' numbers in these chapters are beyond belief, not least in that he gets to a very big figure and then doubles it. It has been calculated that, with 5.3 million men on the move, the first Persian would have arrived in Athens whilst the last man was still not across the Hellespont. Nevertheless, Herodotus does say that this is a calculation, not a guess, and he does have an extraordinarily detailed account of the contingents in his catalogue: see 7.60–100. However, the fault was not that of Herodotus alone: one of the epitaphs for the dead at Thermopylae refers to 3,000,000 Persians (7.228, p. 94) and in other wars and battles the Greeks prove themselves to be very shaky at counting Persians: Xenophon (*Anabasis* 1.8) said that the Persian king had 900,000 soldiers at the battle of Cunaxa in 401 BC, and he was at the battle. For comparison, the total number of soldiers put ashore in Normandy in 1944 during the week after D-Day was 300,000.

Even now scholars can't really agree on a sensible size. However, we aren't always so clever ourselves: demonstrators and police forces can come up with remarkably different figures for the number of people at a protest march.

choinix   1.08 litres.

medimnai   a medimnus is 51.84 litres.

none was more worthy in beauty or stature to hold this power than Xerxes   Xerxes is not simply dismissed by Herodotus as worthless. This remarkable statement about Xerxes' nobility also has echoes of Greek tragedy: we will soon see the fall of this great man.

The battle's preliminaries: 7.201–4, 206–9

7.201   King Xerxes took up his position at Trachis in Malis, and the Greeks took up theirs in the pass. This place is called Thermopylae by most Greeks, but it is called Pylae, the Gates, by the natives and local people. And it was here that both sides took up their positions. The Persian king was in control of all the territory from Trachis to the north and the Greeks were in control of the mainland to the south.   5

7.202   The **Greek forces** who stayed to face the Persian at this place were as follows. There were **300 Spartiates** and 1,000 men from Tegea and Mantinea, half from each, 120 from Orchomenos in Arcadia, an equal number of Arcadians, 400 from Corinth, 200 from Phleious, and 80 from **Mycenae.** These were the contingents from the Peloponnese, but also from Boeotia there were 700 from Thespiae and 10 400 from Thebes.

7.203   In addition to these forces, the people of Opuntian Locris were called out in full force and there were 1,000 from Phocis. The Greeks themselves had called them to participate. They sent the message that this was **just an advance force**, that the rest of the allies were expected any day now and that the sea was guarded and 15 protected by the Athenians and the people of Aegina and others committed to the naval force. They said that there was nothing to fear: 'This is not some god that is attacking Greece, but a man. There is no mortal man for whom there will not be, from the beginning of his life, **a mixture of good and evil: the greater the man, the greater the misfortune.** It must be that, since he is mortal, the invader will fall 20 short of his ambition.' When they heard this, they came to Trachis to help.

Greek forces   even for the Greeks these are very small numbers, particularly in contrast with the Persians. It is worth comparing the size of the Greek forces elsewhere: at the battle of Plataea in 479 BC, there were, according to Herodotus, 38,700 hoplites and 110,000 fighting men in total on the Greek side (9.29–30). The lack of numbers may suggest the uncertainty of the Greeks and the fact that this was merely an advance force.

300 Spartiates   Herodotus tells us that only those with surviving sons were sent (7.205) so that families were not wiped out by death. There is good evidence that throughout the fifth century BC the great warrior Spartans were becoming short of manpower.

Mycenae   Mycenae, 'rich in gold' according to Homer and the site where Heinrich Schliemann made some of the greatest of all archaeological finds, was Agamemnon's home city and a centre of the Mycenaean civilization over a thousand years before Thermopylae. Now it provides 80 men: as Herodotus wrote in 1.5 (p. 7), great cities do become small.

just an advance force   this is another piece of evidence that this was a preliminary force that was taken unawares before support could arrive.

a mixture of good and evil: the greater the man, the greater the misfortune   this concept of the mixture of human fortune is central to Herodotus' account and to the Greek way of thinking.

7.204 Each city had its own general, but it was Leonidas the Spartan **who was most admired** and who led the whole army. He was the son of Anaxandridas, the son of Leon, the son of Eurycratridas, the son of Anaxander, the son of Eurycrates, the son of Polydorus, the son of Alcamenes, the son of Telecles, the son of Archelaus, the son of Agesilaus, the son of Doryssos, the son of Leobotes, the son of Echestratos, the son of Agis, the son of Eurysthenes, the son of Aristodemus, the son of Aristomachus, the son of Cleodaios, the son of Hyllos, the son of **Heracles**.

25

Jacques-Louis David's Leonidas at Thermopylae *was completed in 1814. It shows Leonidas and the Spartan soldiers preparing for the final battle, knowing that they will die. On the left one of the soldiers carves into the rock the Spartans' epitaph whilst three young men dedicate their flower garlands and hence their lives. In the background the Spartans' baggage is taken away to safety.*

who was most admired   Leonidas is to be compared not only with Xerxes (7.186, p. 82) but also, once again, with Homer's *Iliad* 24.629–34, where Priam and Achilles sit together and admire each other's greatness (see note on 1.88). This is a truly heroic and Homeric encounter.

Heracles   see note on 6.116. The Dorians gave legitimacy to their control of the Peloponnese with the myth that the descendants of Heracles, who had been driven out after Heracles' death, later returned to claim their inheritance. Thus the Spartan royal line traced its roots back to Heracles himself. It may be significant that Heracles was said to have died and been cremated on a mountain near Trachis, close to Thermopylae.

7.206 The Spartans sent the men with Leonidas ahead with the intention that the sight of them might encourage the other allies to join the expedition and not go over to the Persians, thinking that the Spartans were being slow to act. The festival of the **Carnea** prevented them from acting at once, but their intention, after the festival had finished, was to send their whole army at once to help, leaving only a defensive garrison in Sparta. The other allies were of the same mind, since at this time also it happened to be the time of the **Olympic Games**. They didn't believe that the battle at Thermopylae would come to a quick resolution so they, too, sent an advance force.

7.207 That was their plan. However, the Persians came up to the pass and **the Greeks at Thermopylae, overcome by fear, were considering escape.** The rest of the soldiers from the Peloponnese wanted to return there and defend the Isthmus, but **the Phocians and the Locrians** were furious at this idea. So Leonidas voted that they should stay where they were and send messengers to all the cities demanding reinforcements, since they would be unable to resist the Persians with such small numbers.

7.208 While they were having these deliberations, Xerxes sent a scout on horseback to see how many the Greeks were and what they were doing. Whilst in Thessaly he had heard that only a small force had been gathered there and that their leaders were the Spartans and Leonidas, the descendant of Heracles. The scout rode up to the camp and took a good, long look. He couldn't see the whole force: the men who were stationed behind the wall they had reconstructed and who were guarding it could not be seen. However, he could see those outside the wall who had left their weapons against the wall. It just happened to be the case that it was

---

Carnea the Carnea was the major Spartan festival held in honour of Apollo Carneius. The same festival is likely to have been the cause of their late arrival at Marathon (6.106, p. 41). The Spartans were famed as much for their religious observance as for their bravery and there are numerous examples of that being a significant factor in their actions: in 9.7 the Spartans cannot act because of the Hyacinthia. On the other hand, it could be argued that, when it suited them, they used religion as an excuse to do what they wanted. There is a further problem, too. If the Spartans were not allowed to fight during this time, why were they allowed to send 300?

Olympic Games this was the greatest of the festivals that involved all the city-states of the Greek world. The traditional date for the founding of the games was 776 BC and they took place every four years in August or September. During the period of the Olympic Games there was a truce between all states to enable people to attend and participate.

the Greeks at Thermopylae, overcome by fear, were considering escape once again there is a suggestion that this force had advanced too far. This sense of uncertainty and even panic runs all the way through to the victory at Salamis.

the Phocians and the Locrians these people would be angry: they are the states immediately south of Thermopylae and retreat by the Greeks from Thermopylae means conquest by the Persians for them.

the Spartans who were stationed there at this time. He could see some of these men exercising and **others combing their hair.** He was amazed at the sight, but he still ascertained the numbers. When he had got all he needed to know accurately, he rode back untroubled. No one pursued him: they just paid him no attention. When he got back he told Xerxes all he had seen.

7.209 When Xerxes heard this report, he couldn't understand at all that they were making preparations, as best they could, to kill or be killed. He thought that their actions were laughable, and he sent for Demaratus who was with the army. When Demaratus arrived Xerxes asked him about everything in detail, hoping to understand the Spartans' actions. Demaratus said, 'I've told you before about these men, when we were setting out against Greece. Then you laughed at me when I told you how I saw that things would turn out. My lord, the hardest challenge for me is to be truthful in your presence. Now listen to me. These men have come here to fight you for this pass and they are making their preparations. This is their custom. Whenever they are about to risk their lives, they comb their hair. You must understand this. If you defeat these men and those who remain in Sparta, there is no other people in the world, my lord, who will take up arms and face you. For at this moment you are facing the finest kingdom in Greece and the best men.'

Demaratus' words seemed absolutely unbelievable to Xerxes and he asked, **for the second time,** how so small a force could fight against his army. Demaratus replied, 'My lord, if things do not turn out as I say, then treat me as a liar.'

The battle: 7.210–25

7.210 Xerxes remained unconvinced by Demaratus' words and for four days he did nothing, always thinking that they would run away. On the fifth day, when they didn't retreat, but instead seemed, by staying put, to be exhibiting both impudence and folly, he grew angry and sent his **Medes and the Cissians** against them. Their orders were to take them alive and bring them into his sight. When the Medes

---

others combing their hair in 1.82 Herodotus tells of the battle of the Champions, a battle between Argos and Sparta in the sixth century BC. In that battle, the two city-states nominated three warriors to fight on each side. After the Spartan victory, the Spartans instituted the custom of wearing their hair long, and the soldiers of Argos of wearing it short. The one surviving Spartan, Othryades, was so ashamed to still be alive that he committed suicide, a precursor of the men of Thermopylae and part of the Spartan myth-making machine.

for the second time Xerxes, like Croesus before him (1.31, p. 11), can't quite understand the first answer he gets, so he asks again.

Medes and the Cissians after the Persians themselves, these were Xerxes' best troops: 7.62 gives an account of their attire.

charged and fell upon the Greeks, many of the Medes fell, but others took up the attack and they didn't retreat, even though they suffered heavy losses. In this engagement they made it clear to anyone, and particularly to the king himself, that he had lots of people, but not many men. **The battle continued throughout the day.**

10

7.211   When the Medes had been roughly handled, they retreated and were replaced in the attack by the Persians under Hydarnes' command. Xerxes called them the Immortals and they thought that they would easily get the job done. In fact, when they engaged with the Spartans, they didn't do any better than the Median army. It was just the same: fighting in a confined space **with spears shorter than the Greeks'**, they couldn't make use of their numerical superiority. The Spartans fought memorably, proving that this was **experts against amateurs**. In particular, one tactic was to turn tail and take to flight *en masse*. At the sight of this flight,

15

the barbarians would charge after them shouting and making a great din. Then, at the very moment when they were caught, the Spartans would turn to face the barbarians, and, having done so, they slaughtered countless numbers of them. However, in this battle there were very few Spartan casualties. Whatever formation they adopted, whatever they did, the Persians couldn't make any progress in their attempt on the pass, and so they withdrew.

20

25

A tile image representing two 'Immortals', the most famous and most feared of Xerxes' troops. They are vividly portrayed here at Susa and in the sculpture and painting of Persepolis. They were called the Immortals because they always numbered 10,000; as one man died, he was replaced by another. For Herodotus' account, see 7.83. Their commander, Hydarnes, was a Persian of very high rank: his father was one of the seven conspirators who killed Smerdis and placed Darius on the throne (3.70).

The battle continued throughout the day   it is striking that all of the engagements with the Persians last as long as a Greek battle can last. There were no easy victories and it was, on each occasion, a close-run thing.

with spears shorter than the Greeks'   one of the key elements of the Greek hoplite's success was the long thrusting spear, over 6 feet (2 metres) in length. The hoplite phalanx presented an impenetrable formation which proved to be superior to Persian methods and weaponry during these years.

experts against amateurs   this is not really fair to the professional Immortals, but Herodotus does attribute greater technical ability to the Greeks in the whole campaign (see his judgement on the battle of Plataea (9.62–3, p. 134)).

7.212 The story is told that the king was watching these attacks and three times **he jumped up out of his seat** in fear for his army. So that was how the battle went on the first day. On the next day the barbarians did no better. They went into battle believing that the enemy, being so small in number, would have taken too many casualties to engage in combat with them. But the Greeks, organized by units and by city-state, took their turn to fight. This did not apply to the Phocians who had been despatched to the mountains to guard the path. So, when the Persians found that things were no different from the day before, they withdrew.

7.213 Xerxes had no idea how to deal with the situation he faced, but then Epialtes, the son of Eurydemus, a man from Malis, came to talk to him in the hope of receiving some great reward from the king. He explained that there was a path that led over the mountain to Thermopylae and thereby he brought about the destruction of the Greeks who stayed to fight.

The Siphnian Treasury is one of many such treasuries built by Greek city-states at Delphi, to house their offerings to Apollo. Siphnos is a small island in the south-western Cyclades, made prosperous by its gold and silver mines. This enabled it to build a treasury at Delphi with a frieze. The scene from this frieze (dated c. 525 BC) is of gods fighting giants, but transposed into a fight involving hoplites. Each hoplite carries his shield in one hand and his spear in the other. The hoplites stand close together, each providing some sort of protection for the next man and forming what was intended to be an impenetrable wall, the phalanx.

---

he jumped up out of his seat as ever Xerxes is the spectator, whereas Leonidas and other Greek leaders fight. Xerxes adopts a similar role at Salamis (see 8.86 (p. 111) and Aeschylus *Persians* 466–7 (p. 118)).

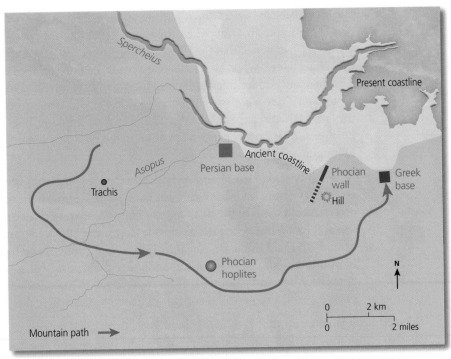

The battle of Thermopylae, 480 BC.

7.215 Xerxes was delighted by what Epialtes promised to do and at once he sent Hydarnes and Hydarnes' men with him. They set out from the camp at about the time of the lighting of the lamps.

7.217 The Persians crossed the river Asopus and marched all night, keeping the mountain of Oitaia on the right and the mountains of Trachis on the left. As dawn appeared, 45 they were on the summit of the mountain. As I made clear before, 1,000 Phocian hoplites were guarding this part of the mountain, protecting their own country and defending the path. The pass below was being guarded by those I have already mentioned, whilst the path was being guarded by volunteers from Phocis, who had taken on the task for Leonidas. 50

7.218 The **Phocians** came to realize that the Persians had reached the summit in the following way. The Persians escaped detection on their ascent because the whole mountain was covered in oak trees. However, it was calm and the soldiers made a great noise, understandably, treading the leaves under foot. So, the Phocians were just getting up and putting on their armour when the Persians were upon them. 55

Phocians this account of events on the mountain above Thermopylae doesn't make much sense. It is possible that Herodotus is relying on a source that puts the best construction on the efforts of the Phocians. Whatever the exact sequence of events, the Phocians did fail to hold the mountain path.

When the Persians saw the men putting on their armour, they were amazed. They had come upon an army when they were expecting no resistance at all. Then Hydarnes, frightened that the Phocians were in fact Spartans, asked Epialtes who the soldiers were. When he was absolutely sure, he lined up the Persians for battle. The Phocians, under thick and constant arrow fire, retreated to the peak of the mountain. They were sure that the assault was directed primarily at them, so they made themselves ready to die. That was their thinking, but the Persians with Epialtes and Hydarnes, paid no attention to the Phocians and descended from the mountain as quickly as possible.

7.219   Amongst the Greeks at Thermopylae it was **the seer Megistias** who, inspecting the sacrificial victims, said that death would come to them with the dawn. Then some deserters told them of the flank march. They passed on this information whilst it was still night, but, when it was already day, some observers ran down from the summit and said the same. Then the Greeks took counsel and they were **divided in opinion**. Some were against abandoning their post, whilst others urged the opposite. Afterwards they parted and some began to leave, each scattering to their own city, whilst those with Leonidas prepared to stay where they were.

7.220   It is also said that Leonidas himself sent them away to ensure that they didn't perish. However, he did not think it right that he and the Spartans with him should abandon the position they had originally come to guard. I am very much of the opinion that Leonidas, realizing that **the allies had lost heart** and did not want to take their share of the danger, ordered them to depart, but he did not think that it was the right thing for him to go. **By staying, he left behind great glory and the good fortune of Sparta was not wiped out.** The Spartans consulted

---

the seer Megistias the Greeks believed that the gods revealed the future through signs, so seers were very important to them. Compare, for example, the role of Tiresias in Sophocles' *Antigone* and *Oedipus the King* and the significance of the sacrificial victims in the timing of the battle of Plataea (9.61, p.133).

divided in opinion at this point Herodotus' version becomes fragmented as he brings together the different accounts of events that inevitably arose. At the heart of the narrative lies the problem that, brave and obedient as the Spartans were, even they would not choose to stay to hold a pass that had already been turned. They were brave, not suicidal.

the allies had lost heart Plutarch (*The Malice of Herodotus* 865b) finds fault with Herodotus for this suggestion, arguing that it reflects Herodotus' personal animosity to the Thebans. However, Plutarch himself is not entirely without prejudice: after all, he came from Thebes.

By staying, he left behind great glory and the good fortune of Sparta was not wiped out one way to explain the decision of Leonidas to stay and die is through the fulfilment of an oracle. Of course, it isn't very difficult to invent an oracle after the event to explain away a disaster and so help a myth to its birth.

---

the oracle at Delphi about the war when it was just stirring and they received the 80
reply that either Sparta would be destroyed by the barbarians or their king would
die. This was the prophecy given to them in **hexameters**:

> For you, dwellers in Sparta of the wide dancing floor,
> Either your great and noble city will be sacked by the **descendants of Perseus**
> Or that will not come to pass, but the land of Lacedaimon   85
> Will lament the death of a king descended from Heracles.
> Neither the strength of bulls or lions will check his might face to face,
> For he has the strength of Zeus. I say that he will not be checked
> Until one of them has been torn to pieces.

I would rather believe that Leonidas took this into consideration and, wanting to 90
lay up **glory** for the Spartans alone, sent the allies away rather than that, divided
in strategy, **they should go their own way in disarray.**

7.221   For me the following is a very important proof that this is what happened.
Megistias, the Acarnanian who was said to be descended from **Melampus**, was the
seer who was with the army and it was he who foretold from the sacrificial victims 95
what was going to happen. When Leonidas sent him away, he did not conceal the
fact that this was so that he didn't die with everyone else. In fact, Megistias didn't
do as he was told, but he sent away his son who was with the army. This was his
only son.

7.222   And so the allies who were sent away left and obeyed Leonidas. The only people 100
who stayed with the Spartans were the Thespians and the Thebans. The Thebans

---

hexameters   the Delphic oracle spoke in hexameters, the metre of epic poetry, especially
Homer's *Iliad* and *Odyssey*. Or rather, the priestess, inspired by Apollo, cried out in an
ecstatic trance and the priests translated her utterances into hexameters for public
consumption.

descendants of Perseus   the Greeks managed to derive the name of the Persians from
Perseus, the child of Zeus and Danaë, who was the slayer of the Gorgon Medusa and the
rescuer of Andromeda.

glory   from Achilles onwards the great motivation for action is glory (see note on p. 2).
However, even Herodotus accepts that there is another version of the narrative: that it
is not glory but dissent and the desire for self-preservation amongst the allies that could
be the important factors.

they should go their own way in disarray   Herodotus may not want to believe this, but
it was clearly a possible – and perhaps common – version of events.

Melampus   a mythical seer who is mentioned in Homer's *Odyssey* (15.225–7), the founder
of the most famous family of seers in the Greek world, the Melampodids.

stayed against their will – **Leonidas kept them there almost as hostages –** whereas the Thespians stayed absolutely willingly. They said that they wouldn't leave Leonidas and his men, but they stayed there and died with them. Their commander was Demophilos, the son of Diadromeus.

105

7.223 At the rising of the sun, Xerxes poured a libation and, at about the time when the market place is at its busiest, he made his attack. Epialtes had told him to do this, since the descent from the mountain is shorter and the terrain is quicker than the

An image from the film 300, *released by Warner Brothers in 2007, based on the graphic novel of the same title written by Frank Miller. The story is a fictionalized version of the Spartans' last stand at Thermopylae. The image shows the Spartan army formed up in a phalanx to defend the pass.*

Leonidas kept them there almost as hostages Plutarch (*The Malice of Herodotus* 865a), once again, can find no logical justification for keeping unwilling fighters there. He believes that it is Herodotus' hatred of Thebes that makes him say this. Presumably these are Thebans who, whatever their city wanted to do, were keen to fight the Persians.

Plutarch (*The Malice of Herodotus* 866a–b) has a yet more glorious account of the Greeks' defeat than that of Herodotus:

> When they learnt in the night of the enemy's journey round behind them, they arose and set out for the Persian camp and the tent of the king, intending to kill him and willing to die in the attempt. Forward they went, right to the tent, killing anyone in their way and routing the rest. When they failed to find Xerxes, they started hunting for him in this huge and sprawling army, and as they roamed around they were hemmed in by the enemy on every side and at last, with difficulty, were slain.

circuitous ascent. The barbarians with Xerxes and the Greeks with Leonidas joined battle. **Indeed Leonidas' men advanced much more than before into the wider part of the neck of the path.** For now they were coming out to fight to the death. On this occasion they joined battle outside the narrows and a great number fell. Behind them, the leaders of each company of Persians **were thrashing all the men with whips,** always urging them onwards. Many of them fell into the sea and were drowned. Even more were trampled under foot by their own men. There is no accurate account of the number of dead. The Greeks knew that death would come to them from those who had come over the mountain, so they showed quite outstanding courage against the enemy and gave no thought to their own survival.

110

115

120

125

This statue of Leonidas was set up in the 1950s by Greeks living in America. It stands opposite the hill of Kolonos, at the very centre of the pass where the Spartans took up their position.

7.224   By this stage in the battle, most of the Greeks had broken their spears so that they were killing the Persians with swords. It was at this point in the struggle that **Leonidas fell, the best of men,** along with other famous Spartans. I found out the names of these men, as being men of great virtue. Indeed, I found out the names 130 of all 300. Amongst the many other famous Persians who died were two sons of Darius, Abrocomes and Hyperanthes, the children of the daughter of Artanes.

Leonidas' men advanced much more than before into the wider part of the neck of the path   this is hard to explain tactically in that they had been so successful in the narrows. Although such speculation is dangerous, it is possible to construct a narrative in which the Spartans, as the rearguard protecting the retreat of the army, are cut off. This advance may be their attempt to fight their way out to safety.

were thrashing all the men with whips   the difference of approach is critical. The Spartans choose to stay even when they know death is inevitable, whereas, even with victory assured, the Persian forces have to be driven into battle.

Leonidas fell, the best of men   just as the *Iliad* has its climaxes in the death of the great warriors, Sarpedon, Patroclus and Hector, so this battle has its climax in the fall of the heroic Leonidas. The similarity is greatest to Hector who chooses to stay outside the walls and fight, even though he knows that it will bring him death (*Iliad* 22.90–2).

The battle of Thermopylae, 480 BC **93**

7.225 **So, two brothers of Xerxes fell fighting** in the **great struggle over the body of Leonidas.** In the end the Greeks managed to drag it away by their courage and routed the enemy four times. This was the situation until the force with Epialtes 135 arrived. When the Greeks realized that they had come, then the nature of the battle changed. They withdrew again into the narrow part of the pass, crossed the wall and all of them, except the Thebans, took up their position, all together, on the hill. The hill is at the entrance, where now the stone lion stands in honour of Leonidas. They defended this place with the knives that some of them still 140 had with them, with their bare hands and even with their teeth as the Persians showered them with arrows. Some of the barbarians pursued them and broke down the defensive wall, whilst others just stood all around them.

The glorious dead: 7.226–8, 238

7.226 Of all the Spartans and the Thespians who fought in this way, it is said that the Spartan Dieneces was the finest in battle. They say that he proved this even before they joined battle with the Medes. He heard from one of the soldiers from Trachis that, when the barbarians fired off their arrows, they were so dense that they hid the sun, so great was their number. He, not at all disturbed by such words 5 and paying no regard to the numbers of the Persians, replied that his Trachinian friend was bringing good news: 'If the Medes block out the sun, then we will fight in the shade, not in the sun.' They say that Dieneces the Spartan **said many other things like this** and left them as his memorial.

7.227 They say that the next best men after him were two brothers, Alpheo and Maron, 10 the sons of Orisphates. The man given the highest regard by the Thespians was Dithryambus, the son of Armatides.

7.228 **They were buried where they fell** and for those who had died before Leonidas sent them away to safety, the following inscription was set up:

HERE FOUR THOUSAND PELOPONNESIANS FOUGHT AGAINST THREE MILLION MEN. 15

So, two brothers of Xerxes fell fighting   Xerxes may be safe from danger in this war, but his relations die like everyone else.

great struggle over the body of Leonidas   here life imitates art in that the scene recalls the great fights in Homer's *Iliad* over the corpses of Sarpedon (16.550–675) and Patroclus (17.1–761).

said many other things like this   this is the finest of that rare thing, a Spartan joke. However, Plutarch does preserve some sayings of the Spartans, most of which are characterized by their brevity and dry wit and embody the Spartans' heroism and total dedication to their city (for one example see 3.46). *Plutarch on Sparta* (pp. 109–63) is well worth reading.

They were buried where they fell   the honour that was given to Tellos in Croesus' story (1.30, p. 11) and to the Athenians at Marathon.

This is the inscription for all those who died, but there was a separate inscription for the Spartans:

STRANGER, TELL THE SPARTANS THAT WE LIE HERE, OBEDIENT TO THEIR COMMANDS.

That was the inscription for the Spartans, but there was also this for the seer Megistias: 20

THIS IS THE TOMB OF FAMOUS MEGISTIAS, WHOM THE MEDES KILLED, CROSSING THE RIVER SPERCHEIOS. HE WAS A SEER, WHO KNEW CLEARLY THAT DEATH WAS COMING UPON HIM, BUT HE DID NOT DARE DESERT THE LEADERS OF SPARTA.

The Amphictyons honoured these men with the inscriptions and tombstone,   25
except the inscription for the seer. **Simonides**, the son of Leoprepes, wrote the verse for the seer Megistias for reasons of **guest-friendship**.

7.238   Xerxes walked amongst the corpses. He had heard that Leonidas was the king and the general of the Spartans and he gave the command that **his head should be cut off and set on a stake.** This is an important piece of evidence – and there is a great   30
deal more – that Leonidas was a greater cause of anger for Xerxes than any other man alive. Otherwise, he would not have committed such a dreadful outrage to his corpse since, of all peoples that I know of, the Persians do the greatest honour to those who fight bravely. Those who had been told to do this carried out their orders.   35

Stranger, tell the Spartans   the most famous of all military epitaphs. Compare the epitaph written in the First World War by J. M. Edmonds, who was a classical scholar:

> When you go home, tell them of us and say
> For your tomorrows these gave their to-day.

In turn, this was adapted as an epitaph for the British dead at the battle of Kohima in Burma in 1944.

The Amphictyons   a confederation of peoples who occupied this area. The name means 'those who live round about' (see 7.200). They were also the governing body of the oracle of Apollo at Delphi (see the entry 'amphictiony' in the *Oxford Classical Dictionary*).

Simonides   one of the most famous of poets at the end of the sixth and beginning of the fifth century BC. None of his longer poems survives intact, but there are substantial fragments, including some, recently discovered, from his poem on the battle of Plataea. He was, perhaps, most famous for his funeral epigrams, like this one.

guest-friendship   for the concept of guest-friendship, see the note on 7.29.

his head should be cut off and set on a stake   impalement is presented as the Persians' most brutal way to treat the dead: Darius impaled 3,000 Babylonians (3.159); Polycrates, the tyrant of Samos (3.125), and Histiaeus of Miletus (6.31) suffered a similar fate. After the battle of Plataea the Spartan leader Pausanias refused to impale Mardonius, the Persian leader (9.78–9, p. 140). Such treatment may also echo Achilles' abuse of the corpse of Hector in *Iliad* 22.

1. On what does Herodotus' narrative of Thermopylae concentrate?
2. How does Herodotus make the narrative exciting, dramatic, moving?
3. What are the different sources that are visible in Herodotus' account?
4. What does the dialogue between Xerxes and Demaratus contribute?
5. Why does Herodotus include the epitaphs?
6. What do we think of Herodotus' numbers?
7. Can a different narrative of this event be constructed?
8. How does Herodotus bring out the difference between the Greeks and the Persians?
9. What echoes are there of Homer in this narrative? What do they contribute?
10. Investigate other historical examples of disaster dressed up as glory.

7 The battle of Salamis, 480 BC

After the defeat at Thermopylae, the Greek forces were forced to withdraw south towards the Isthmus of Corinth, the next obvious place to make a stand. Therefore, many Greek states were overrun, including Athens itself. The Persians captured Athens and set fire to the Acropolis, burning the temples there in revenge for the sack of Sardis in 499 BC (5.100–2). It is still possible to see, set into the side of the Acropolis, the fire-scorched column drums from that attack. The Athenians fled the city, some crossing to Troezen on the Peloponnese (see map on p. 9), some to the islands, Aegina in the Saronic Gulf and Salamis, tucked in close against the coast of Attica. As ever, there was a **difference of opinion** amongst the Greeks. The Athenians, led by Themistocles, wanted to fight in the narrows between the island of Salamis and the mainland, thereby protecting their people and possessions. The cities of the Peloponnese were much more interested in retreating to the natural defensive line of the Isthmus (8.49). The Athenians had great influence because of the size of their fleet, but the overall command was still in the hands of the Spartan Eurybiades.

The debate amongst the Greeks at Salamis: 8.56–63

8.56   When news came to the Greeks at Salamis of what had happened on the Acropolis at Athens, they were thrown into such a **state of panic** that some of the generals didn't even wait for the **proposed plan** to be approved, but rushed to their ships and hoisted sail to flee. Those who did stay approved the plan to fight in defence of the Isthmus. As night fell, the meeting broke up and they embarked on their ships.   5

---

difference of opinion this debate has two significant echoes. The first is with the debate in Homer *Iliad* 2.53–153, where Agamemnon unintentionally causes a flight to the ships. The problem is solved by Odysseus, at the prompting of Athena, just as the problem amongst the Greeks is solved by Themistocles at the urging of Mnesiphilos. The second parallel is with the battle of Marathon, where Miltiades, unsuccessful in discussion, went to the polemarch, Callimachus, and persuaded him to support his plan (6.109, pp. 42–3).

state of panic Herodotus' account is not very flattering to the Greeks. They are divided and prone to panic throughout. Such capacity for disagreement goes back as far as 4.137 when the Ionians, left by Darius to guard the bridge over the Danube, can't agree on what to do.

proposed plan the plan would involve withdrawal to the Isthmus.

8.57   When **Themistocles** returned to his ship, **Mnesiphilos**, an Athenian, asked Themistocles what had been decided. When Themistocles told him that it had been decided to sail to the Isthmus and to fight a sea battle in defence of the Peloponnese, Mnesiphilos said, 'No, no! If they take their ships away from Salamis, you will no longer be fighting for one country. Everyone will return to his own city. Neither **Eurybiades** nor anyone else will be able to stop the fragmentation of the army. Greece will perish by its own acts of folly. But, if there is any way at all, go and try to confound their plans. See if, somehow or other, you can persuade Eurybiades to change his plan and stay here.' *(10)*

8.58   Themistocles really liked this idea and, making no reply, he went to Eurybiades' *(15)* ship. When he got there, he said that he wanted to share with him a matter of common interest. Eurybiades invited him on board and told him to say what he wanted. Then Themistocles sat down and told Eurybiades everything that Mnesiphilos had said, **pretending that it was his own idea**. He also added lots of other arguments until he convinced him to go back on shore and call a meeting *(20)* of the generals.

8.59   When the generals were all gathered and before Eurybiades could explain the reason for the meeting, Themistocles went for it, as a man does when he is making

---

Themistocles the major Athenian politician at the beginning of the fifth century BC. As archon in 493/2 he was responsible for developing the harbour at Piraeus and in 483 it was on his advice that the Athenians decided to spend the silver found at Laurium on enlarging the Athenian fleet, the key decision that brought victory in 480.

Mnesiphilos according to Plutarch, he was Themistocles' teacher. He was once thought to be fictional, but twelve ostraka, pieces of pottery used to vote for the expulsion or 'ostracism' – ten-year exile – of a citizen, have now been found in Athens (see the illustration on p. 109). Here, as often, Herodotus turns out to be right, unexpectedly.

Eurybiades Eurybiades has been in command of the fleet at Artemisium and is in charge here even though the Spartans were famously warriors on land and had no substantial fleet. They provide only 16 ships at Salamis whereas, according to Herodotus, the Athenians provided 180 out of a contingent of 378. Although the Athenians provided so many ships, the other Greeks refused to serve under the Athenians.

pretending that it was his own idea although Themistocles is the hero of the Athenians, Herodotus is not averse to painting him as a crafty, duplicitous character. At Artemisium (8.4–5) he took a bribe of 30 talents from the Euboeans to keep the fleet there and then used 5 talents of it to bribe Eurybiades and 3 talents of it to bribe Adeimantus to stay. The Greeks admired the trickery of Homer's Odysseus, the man of many wiles, as much as the courage of Achilles.

a big demand. As he was speaking, **Adeimantus**, the son of Okytos, the Corinthian general, said, 'Themistocles, **in a race those who make a false start are whipped.** 25 'Yes, but those who get left behind don't win any prizes,' retorted Themistocles.

8.60   On this occasion Themistocles gave a gentle reply to the Corinthian. In his speech Themistocles didn't use any of the arguments that he had used before to Eurybiades – that if they left Salamis the fleet would scatter. It wasn't appropriate to make such an accusation in the presence of the allies. **This time he used a** 30 **different argument** and said: '**This is your chance to save Greece**, if you follow my advice and stay and fight here rather than, on the advice of others, withdraw the ships to the Isthmus. Consider the two alternatives. First, at the Isthmus we will be fighting on the open sea. That puts us at a serious disadvantage, since we have **heavier ships** but fewer of them. Secondly, even if we are successful, you will 35 lose Salamis and Megara and Aegina. Thirdly, their land forces will keep pace with the fleet, so you will be bringing them into the Peloponnese and putting the whole of Greece at risk.

'On the other hand, if you do as I say, you will find that there are very many advantages. First, if we fight in the narrows, even though outnumbered, we will, in 40 all probability, win a great victory. For a battle in the narrows is to our advantage, a battle in the open sea is to theirs. Secondly, Salamis will survive and it is there that we have placed our women and children for their safety. And there is this final point, which is of the greatest concern to you. Whether you fight here or at the Isthmus, you will be fighting in defence of the Peloponnese, and you won't 45 draw them on to the Peloponnese, if you've got any sense. If things turn out as I hope and we win a victory at sea, the barbarians will not pass over to the Isthmus and they won't advance any further than Attica. They will retreat in disarray and

---

Adeimantus   the tension between the Athenians and the Corinthians and the personal animosity between Themistocles and Adeimantus are key elements in the battle. Herodotus clearly has one version of events that is firmly anti-Corinthian.

in a race those who make a false start are whipped   such was the punishment in the Olympic Games for cheats. Pithy quotations would have been preserved, just as the words of Wellington, Churchill, Lincoln and J. F. Kennedy are passed down. Themistocles is not a good man to take on in repartee (see Plutarch *Themistocles* 18.2–5).

This time he used a different argument   Themistocles the wise adapts his argument to the moment and the people who hear it.

This is your chance to save Greece   this is very much the argument used by Miltiades at Marathon (6.109, p. 43). He appeals to the nobility of the cause and produces practical reasons: he does not use the negative arguments that Mnesiphilos originally offered.

heavier ships   the trireme, which formed the greater part of the Athenian fleet, was a very large vessel in the context of the times. It was rowed by 170 men on three tiers and it relied upon its speed and power as a ramming machine (see the illustration on p. 110). The Persian fleet was much lighter and more manoeuvrable.

The temple to Apollo at Delphi stands on the slopes of Mount Parnassus, overlooking the Krisaean plain that lies below, covered in olive trees. In this temple, built in the late sixth century BC, the Pythian priestess gave her prophecies.

we will benefit from the survival of Megara and Aegina and Salamis. **The oracle speaks of Salamis as the place where we will get the better of our enemies. We must, as men, plan according to what is likely to happen.** If we don't do that, god is not going to lend his support to our human plans.' 50

The oracle as the Persian forces approached Athens, the Delphic oracle's advice was deeply pessimistic and, typically, riddling and ambiguous. The first answer (7.140) began:

> Fools, why sit you here? Fly to the end of the earth.
> Leave your homes and the lofty heights girded by your city.

When the Athenians asked again, the second answer (7.141) was not much better:

> While all else that lies within the borders of Cecrops' [founder of
>   Athens] land
> And the vale of holy Cithaeron [mountain above Thebes] is falling
>   to the enemy,
> Far-seeing Zeus gives you, Tritogeneia [Athena], a wall of wood.
> Only this will stand intact and help you and your children.
> Divine Salamis, you will be the death of mothers' sons
> Either when the seed is scattered or when it is gathered in.

However, it was Themistocles' genius to interpret it correctly. The 'wooden wall' was not the ancient wall around Athens, but the wooden walls of the fleet, and Salamis may be a place of death, but it is 'divine', and therefore a good thing (7.140–4).

We must, as men, plan according to what is likely to happen here we have the realist and pragmatic leader in a world that is not just divinely driven or controlled by chance. We also see Themistocles employing the 'argument from probability', a key Greek rhetorical strategy. Artemisia does the same in 8.68 (pp. 104–5). It is the mark of the intelligent adviser.

8.61 As Themistocles was speaking, the Corinthian Adeimantus once again attacked him. He told Themistocles to shut up since he had no city, and he told Eurybiades not to allow a stateless man to make a proposal. 'Once you've got a city, then you can have some opinions,' he told Themistocles. He made this point because Athens had been captured and was in enemy hands. It was at this moment that **Themistocles poured much abuse** on Adeimantus and the Corinthians, and he made it absolutely clear to them that he had a greater city and country than they did as long as Athens had 200 ships manned with her own men: they could easily see off any Greek state that attacked them.

8.62 Having made his point clear, he turned to Eurybiades and spoke **with even more urgency**. 'If you stay here, you will thereby show yourself to be a great man. If you don't, Greece will be overthrown because of you. All of this war depends on the ships. So do as I tell you. If you don't, we will just go, pick up our people and sail off to **Siris** in Italy. Siris has been ours from a long time ago, and oracles tell us that we should colonize it. All of you, when you have lost allies like this, will remember my words.'

8.63 Themistocles' speech changed Eurybiades' mind. In my opinion, the most important factor in the change was his fear that the Athenians would leave them if they sailed to the Isthmus. If they left, the rest of the Greek forces would no longer be a match for the enemy. So he supported the proposal to stay where they were and fight it out there.

Themistocles poured much abuse very different from the 'debates' in the court of the Persian king. Themistocles is quite willing to use argument, abuse, threats, trickery and bribery to achieve his ends. There is an obvious contrast between the servility of the Persian advisers, who only offer agreement, and the freedom of speech of which the Athenians were so proud in their democracy.

with even more urgency Themistocles' speech here is marked by sharp, staccato sentences, reflecting the urgency of the moment.

Siris the Greek world did not just consist of mainland Greece, or even mainland Greece and Ionia. In the previous three centuries, the Greeks had colonized much of the Mediterranean coast, living, as Plato puts it (*Phaedo* 109b), like frogs around a pond. In particular they had colonized Sicily and southern Italy, which is why some of the best surviving ancient Greek sites (e.g. Agrigento and Paestum) are there. Thus, the idea of migrating to Siris, on the instep of Italy, is not such an impossible idea. After all, Athens was lost. There are other signs of Athenian links to the west: Themistocles' own children were called Italia and Sybaris (a colony in southern Italy) and in the 440s BC the Athenians did found a colony at Thurii, not far from Siris. Herodotus was said to have taken part in that colonization, and Aristotle (*Rhetoric* 3.9) calls him 'Herodotus of Thurii'.

The sons of Aeacus and the Eleusinian Mysteries: 8.64–5

8.64   And so, **after this verbal skirmishing**, once Eurybiades had made his decision, they made ready for battle. On the next day, at sunrise, there was an earthquake which was felt both on land and at sea. The Greeks decided to pray to the gods and to call the **sons of Aeacus** to be their allies. That was their decision, and at once they set about it. They prayed to all the gods and they called Ajax and Telamon   5 from Salamis itself to help, and they sent a ship to Aegina to bring Aeacus and his other sons.

8.65   Dicaeus, the son of Theocydes, who was an Athenian in exile from Athens and was highly respected by the Persians, told the following story. He said that at this time, when the land of Attica was being plundered by Xerxes' land forces and the   10 country was empty of Athenians, he happened to be with the Spartan Demaratus on the **Thriasian plain**. They saw a dust cloud coming from **Eleusis**, as if there were a crowd of **30,000 men**. They were wondering who could have made such a dust cloud and at once, they heard a cry, and it seemed to them to be the cry of the Mysteries, 'Iacchus'. Now, Demaratus was unacquainted with the rites that   15

---

after this verbal skirmishing   Herodotus writes literally 'having thrown spears at each other'.

sons of Aeacus   Aeacus is the son of Zeus and Aegina and the mythical king of Aegina. He had two sons, Telamon, the father of Ajax and Teucer, and Peleus, the father of Achilles. Ajax, who was king of Salamis, was the second best fighter for the Greeks at Troy after Achilles. The Greeks had great faith in the physical power and presence of heroes, so that these images will have been carried into battle as a talisman. For example, the recovery of the great bones of Orestes was a key moment in Spartan history (1.67–8) and the Athenian general Cimon gained great honour by bringing back the bones of Theseus (Plutarch, *Cimon* 8). This might also be compared with the veneration of relics in the Christian tradition.

Thriasian plain   the plain between Athens and Eleusis.

Eleusis   this is a phantom procession to Eleusis. The Eleusinian Mysteries were one of the most sacred rites in the Greek world and were preceded by a 15-mile procession down the Sacred Way from Athens to Eleusis. The Mysteries were held in honour of Demeter, the goddess of the earth and fertility, and her daughter, Persephone, who spends some of her life in the upper world, the time of fertility, and the rest of her time in the underworld, the time of winter and death. Although many of the details still remain obscure, initiation in the Mysteries was meant to offer some form of life after death. Here, as elsewhere, the gods and heroes come to the aid of the city with which they are particularly associated.

30,000 men   the figure of 30,000 is significant in that it is Herodotus' estimate (5.97), and that of others, for the citizen population of Athens.

Iacchus   the day of the procession from Athens to Eleusis was called Iacchus after the ritual cry raised by the worshippers. Iacchus is the patron god of the procession and the name is closely linked as a cult title to Dionysus/Bacchus.

took place at Eleusis. So he asked Dicaeus what the sound was. Dicaeus replied, 'Demaratus, it is inevitable that a great ruin will come upon the king's army. It is absolutely clear. Attica is deserted, so this sound must come from the gods, from Eleusis, to bring **vengeance** for the Athenians and their allies. If it falls upon the Peloponnese, then the danger will come to the king himself and his land forces. If it turns towards the ships at Salamis, then the king runs the risk of losing his fleet. The Athenians hold this festival every year to the Mother **Demeter and her daughter**, and all Athenians and all Greeks can be initiated into the Mysteries. And the cry you hear is the cry of "Iacchus" that they make in this festival.' Demaratus replied, 'Be quiet. Say nothing to anyone about all this. If your words reached the king, you'd lose your head and neither I nor anyone else in the world could save you. Say nothing. The fate of the expedition will be in the hands of the gods.' This was his advice. After the dust and sounds there came a cloud and, rising up, it passed towards Salamis and the camp of the Greeks. In this way they learned that Xerxes' fleet would be destroyed. This is what Dicaeus, the son of Theocydes, used to say and he claimed as witnesses of this Demaratus and others, too.

The situation amongst the Persians: Artemisia's advice: 8.66–9

8.66   After the men in Xerxes' fleet had been to see the slaughter of the Spartans [at Thermopylae], they crossed over from Trachis to Histiaea. They waited there for three days and then sailed through the **Euripus to Phaleron**, arriving there a further three days later. In my opinion, the numbers that attacked Athens by land and sea were no smaller than those that arrived at Sepias and Thermopylae. I calculate that those who were killed by the storm or at Thermopylae or in the sea battles at Artemisium were replaced by those who had not yet joined the king's forces, men from Malia and Doris and Boeotia – who came out in full force apart from the Thespians and Plataeans – and particularly the men from **Carystus, Andros, Tenos** and all the other men from the islands, apart from **the five city-states** I named earlier. For the further the Persian advanced into Greece, the more peoples followed him.

---

vengeance   presumably the gods are taking vengeance on the Persians for their arrogance in aiming to conquer Greece, or for their burning of the temples of Athens. Vengeance is seen by Herodotus as one of the factors of causation that form his narrative.

Demeter and her daughter   see note (p. 102) on Eleusis.

Euripus to Phaleron   Euripus is the narrow channel between Euboea and the mainland, and Phaleron was, at this time, the main harbour of the Athenians (see map on p. 108).

Carystus, Andros, Tenos   Carystus is a town on Euboea; Andros and Tenos are two islands, part of the Cyclades in the Aegean (see map on p. 9).

the five city-states   in 8.46 Herodotus refers to six islands who did not support Xerxes: Ceos, Naxos, Cythnos, Seriphos, Siphnos (see p. 88) and Malos. Herodotus seems to have forgotten one of the six here.

8.67 So when all these people had arrived in Athens – apart from the Parians, who had been left behind on Kythnos and were waiting to see how the war turned out – and everyone else had gone to Phaleron, at that point Xerxes came down in person to the ships, wanting to be with his forces and find out what they thought. When he got there, Xerxes took his seat. The rulers of their own contingents and the naval commanders who had been sent for were present. They sat in order, according to the rank that the king had given to each. First was the king of Sidon, then the king of Tyre, and then everyone else. And when they were all sitting in order, Xerxes sent Mardonius to ask each one of them whether he should fight a sea battle.

8.68 Mardonius went round and asked them all in turn, starting with the king of Sidon, and **everyone offered the same opinion**, telling him to fight a sea battle. But **Artemisia** spoke as follows: 'Mardonius, tell the king for me that this is what I say. He should remember that my actions were not the worst or the least in the sea battles off Euboea. Tell him, "Master, it is only right that I should give you my true opinion, what I believe to be for the best in your present situation. I tell you this: spare your ships and don't fight a sea battle. For at sea their men are as much superior to yours **as men are to women**. Anyway, why is it so vital that you should take a risk in fighting at sea? Don't you possess Athens, the purpose of your mission? Don't you have the rest of Greece? No one stands in your way. Those who resisted you got their deserts. I'll tell you how I think things will turn out for those who have opposed you. If you don't rush into a sea battle, but keep your ships and either stay put or even advance to the Peloponnese, you'll easily get what you came for. For the Greeks can't put up resistance for long, but you'll scatter them and they will all run off to their own cities. As I understand it, they don't have any supplies on this island. And if you lead your land forces against the Peloponnese, it's not **likely** that those of the forces that have come from there will stay where they are and do nothing or be bothered about fighting a sea battle in defence of Athens.

---

everyone offered the same opinion Herodotus' narrative of this debate is to be compared not only with the Greek way of debate, but also with the previous discussions Xerxes has had before and during the campaign with Artabanus (7.11 (pp. 58–9), 7.46–52 (pp. 69–73)) and Demaratus (7.101–5, pp. 75–8). Here there is deference and distance between those involved and no chance of anyone saying what they really think.

Artemisia Artemisia was the daughter of Lygdamis, the tyrant of Halicarnassus, Herodotus' home city. She gets a great deal of coverage and Herodotus says at her first appearance (7.99) that this is because she is unique as a female commander who did great things. However, it is also true that Artemisia was the ruler of Halicarnassus, so Herodotus would not have been short of material. She is a memorable figure, one of the few to offer good advice to Xerxes.

as men are to women an ironic comment from a woman. Nevertheless, Xerxes seems to remember the comparison and uses it for himself in 8.88 (p. 112).

likely Artemisia shows her intelligence by using probability as a means of planning for the future. Compare the words of Themistocles (8.60, p. 100).

But if you rush into a sea battle straightaway, I am afraid that the naval force will 40
be defeated and take the land force down with it. And, there's another thing, your
majesty, you should ponder in your heart. Good men tend to have bad **slaves** and
vice versa. Since you are the best of all men, you have bad slaves. There are some
people, men from Egypt and Cyprus and Cilicia and Pamphylia, who are counted
as your allies, but are no use.'" 45

8.69   As she was making her speech, those who were sympathetic to Artemisia thought
that it would be a disaster and that she might suffer some punishment from the
king, because she was stopping him from fighting a sea battle. On the other hand,
those who bore a grudge against her or envied her because she was honoured
amongst the very best of the allies, were pleased that her reply was going to ruin her. 50
However, when these views were reported to Xerxes, he was absolutely delighted
by Artemisia's advice, and, although before he had a high regard for her, now he
praised her even more. Even so, he gave the command that the **opinion of the
majority** should be followed. He had come to the conclusion that his men had
deliberately fought badly off Euboea because **he hadn't been there**; this time, he 55
had made sure that he was there himself to watch them fight.

The Greeks before the battle: 8.70–82

8.70   When the king had given the order to put to sea, they set sail for Salamis and
were able to take up their different stations without difficulty. By this stage of the
day there wasn't time to engage in fighting; night had come upon them, so they
made preparation to fight the next day. Fear and trepidation took possession of the
Greeks, and especially those from the Peloponnese. They were frightened that they 5
were stuck on Salamis about to fight a sea battle for Athenian territory, but, if they
were defeated, they would be trapped and besieged on the island, leaving their own
country unprotected.

8.71   During that night the Persian land army marched in the direction of the
Peloponnese. However, everything possible had been done to ensure that the 10

---

slaves Artemisia views Xerxes' troops as slaves, whereas the Greeks are all free men
fighting for their own cities. Artemisia's analysis reflects the Greeks' (and Herodotus')
perception of the difference between themselves and their enemy, and it is a reason,
they believe, for their ultimate victory.

opinion of the majority   it is ironic that this is a moment when democracy is in action
in the Persian court and Xerxes, by following the majority, gets it wrong. Artabanus'
wisdom was similarly ignored, but for different reasons (7.12–18, pp. 59–62).

he hadn't been there   Xerxes thinks that his very presence is enough. Indeed, it did
make them fight harder at Salamis (8.86, p. 111), but it didn't make things any better.
The different qualities of Miltiades, Leonidas and Themistocles make it clear that leaders
can make a difference not only by their presence, but by their intelligence and by their
example.

Persians could not invade by land. As soon as the Peloponnesians had learned of the death of Leonidas' men at Thermopylae, they had rushed from all their cities and taken up their positions at the **Isthmus**. Their commander was **Cleombrotus**, the son of Anaxandridas, the brother of Leonidas. When they had taken up their position at the Isthmus and demolished the **Scironian road**, they consulted and decided to build a wall across the Isthmus. Since there were tens of thousands there and everyone worked at it, it was being brought to completion. They brought stones and slabs and pieces of wood and baskets full of sand, and those who had come to help didn't rest from their labours by night or day.

8.72 The following Greeks came in full force to the Isthmus to help: men from Sparta, Arcadia – with every man they had – and Elis and Corinth and Sicyon and Epidaurus and Phleia and Troezen and Hermione. These were the people who came to help, being deeply afraid for Greece in its moment of peril. None of the other Peloponnesians were bothered to do anything, even though the Olympic festival and the Carnea were now finished.

8.74 So the Greeks at the Isthmus got on with their job. They knew that everything was at stake in this race and they didn't expect that the fleet would cover itself in glory. The men on Salamis knew what they were doing, but, even so, they were frightened, not so much for themselves as for the Peloponnese. **For some time people were whispering**, each man to his neighbour, expressing amazement at the folly of Eurybiades. In the end, this all broke out into the open, so there was a meeting and a lot of time was spent on the old arguments. Some said that they should sail to the Peloponnese and take their chance there and certainly not stay and fight for territory that was already lost. The people of Athens and Aegina and Megara were in favour of staying and fighting where they were.

8.75 At this point Themistocles realized that he was losing the argument to the Peloponnesians, so **he slipped out of the meeting** unnoticed and sent a man

---

Isthmus   at its narrowest the Isthmus is four miles across.

Cleombrotus   after the death of Leonidas at Thermopylae, Cleombrotus, his brother, became one of the two kings of Sparta.

Scironian road   the road that runs from Attica through Megara towards the Isthmus and the Peloponnese. As in modern-day warfare, the destruction of roads and bridges is a key tactic, especially in a mountainous area like Greece. The Scironian road is named after the mythical brigand Sciron, who asked travellers to wash his feet and then kicked them into the sea. He was one of the threats to society dealt with by Theseus in his labours, an imitation (and pale shadow) of Heracles' achievements.

For some time people were whispering   whatever Herodotus' inadequacies as a military historian, his account is psychologically persuasive: the nervous talking in the camp and the return to old arguments.

he slipped out of the meeting   Themistocles has no scruples and will deceive anyone, as long as it achieves his ends.

by ship to the Persian camp. He told him what he had to say. The man's name was Sicinnus, a house slave and the **teacher** of Themistocles' children. After all this was over Themistocles made him a citizen of **Thespiae** – at that time the 40 Thespians were looking for citizens – and he made him a wealthy man, too. When he arrived by ship, Sicinnus made the following speech to the barbarians' generals. 'The general of the Athenians has sent me to you without the knowledge of the other Greeks. It happens to be the case that he is sympathetic to the Persian king and would prefer a Persian victory to a Greek victory. I am here to tell you that 45 the Greeks are in a state of panic and are planning flight. Now is your chance to perform the finest of all deeds if you don't allow them to escape. They are at odds with each other and they won't resist you any further. You'll see them fighting against each other, those who are sympathetic to you and those who are not.' This was Sicinnus' message and, when he had delivered it, he got out of the way. 50

8.76   The Persians believed this report to be reliable, so the first thing they did was land many soldiers on the small island of **Psyttaleia**, which lies between Salamis and the mainland. Then, at midnight, the western wing of the fleet set sail on an encircling movement towards Salamis while the other wing on the side near **Ceos** and **Cynosoura** set sail and occupied the whole channel as far as **Munichia** 55 with their ships. Their reason for these moves was to prevent the Greeks from flight and, having trapped them at Salamis, to pay them back for their exploits at Artemisium. They put the men on the island of Psyttaleia for the following reason. They thought that, when the battle took place, this island, being in the straits where the battle would happen, would be the place on which most of the 60 men and shipwrecks would wash up. So they would be able to help their own men and kill the enemy. They did all of these things in silence so that the enemy would not find out about them. And so they got no sleep that night.

8.78   There was still a **war of words** going on between the generals at Salamis. They did not yet know that the barbarians had completely encircled them with their ships; 65 they imagined that they were still in the place where they had seen them to be during the day.

---

teacher   the Greeks employed their domestic slaves to supervise the education of their young children.

Thespiae   this city near Thebes and Plataea in Boeotia needed new citizens, having lost 700 at Thermopylae (7.202, 222, pp. 83, 91–2).

Psyttaleia, Ceos, Cynosoura, Munichia   there isn't absolute agreement about the exact location of the first three of these – the map on p. 108 presents one possibility. The Ceos mentioned here is *not* the island in the Cyclades to the east of Cape Sounion.

war of words   as in 8.64 (p. 102), Herodotus deliberately uses military vocabulary to describe the argument. 'War of words' is a translation of the Greek word that is used for the forward surge and push that takes place at the critical moment of a hoplite battle.

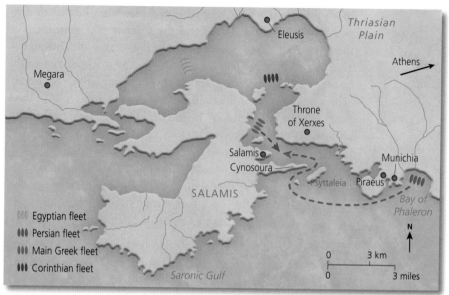

The battle of Salamis, 480 BC.

8.79   While the generals were still fighting, **Aristides**, the son of Lysimachus, crossed over from Aegina. He was an Athenian, but he had been **ostracized** by the people. I have learnt about his character and I have come to the judgement that he was 70 the best and the most honourable man in Athens. This man came to the meeting place and asked for Themistocles; he was no friend of his. Indeed he was his greatest enemy. However, the scale of the crisis led him to forget this and ask for Themistocles, wanting to talk to him. He had already heard that the generals from the Peloponnese were eager to set sail for the Isthmus. When Themistocles 75 came out, Aristides spoke as follows: 'We must strive at any time, but above all now, to see which of us can bring the most benefit to our country. I tell you that it makes no difference whether the Peloponnesians say a lot or a little about sailing away from here. I am an eye-witness of this and I say that the Corinthians and Eurybiades himself couldn't sail away, even if they wanted to. We are entirely 80 surrounded by the enemy. Go in and tell them this.'

8.80   Themistocles replied: 'Your advice is excellent and you have brought good news. You have come here as an eye-witness of the very things that I wanted to happen.

Aristides   Aristides was an important figure in Athenian history both before and after the Persian Wars. In particular, he was the main architect of the Delian League, the defensive Aegean alliance constructed by the Greeks after the defeat of the Persians.

ostracized   in 486 BC Aristides had been ostracized by the Athenian people. This was a constitutional process through which the Athenians could send into exile for ten years, without any specific charge, anyone they didn't want to be around. Plutarch *Aristides* 7 tells a wonderful story of Aristides helping an illiterate fellow Athenian to vote for his own exile by writing his own name on an ostrakon.

Ostrakon with the name of Aristides, the son of Lysimachus. In the Athenian system of ostracism, every citizen had the right to write on a piece of pot, an ostrakon, the name of the person whom they wanted to be exiled for ten years. Many such ostraka have been found, mainly in the Agora at Athens, and this one of Aristides dates from the years immediately after the Persian Wars.

You should know that I was the reason for the Persians' actions. The Greeks wouldn't face battle of their own free will, so it had to be that they did it against 85 their will. You have come here with the good news, so tell them yourself. If I tell them, they'll think that I've made it up and they won't believe that the barbarians are doing this. No, you go and tell them how it is. And if they do believe what you tell them, all well and good. If they don't, it will make no difference to us. They still won't be able to run away, if we are surrounded on all sides, as you say.' 90

8.81   So Aristides went in and told them. He said that he had come from Aegina and barely been able to get through the blockade unseen: the whole of the Greek fleet was surrounded by the ships of Xerxes. His advice was that they should make preparations to defend themselves. Having made his report, Aristides left, but once again there was an argument. The majority of the generals didn't believe the 95 report.

8.82   But while they were still in their state of disbelief, a trireme from **Tenos**, which was deserting from the Persians, commanded by a Tenian called Panaitios, the son of Sosimenes, brought the whole truth. For this act the names of the Tenians were written at Delphi on the **tripod** amongst those who had destroyed the barbarian. 100 With this ship that deserted at Salamis and the Lemnian ship that deserted before at Artemisium the Greek fleet reached the total of 380. Until then they had been two short of that number.

Tenos   an island north of Delos in the middle of the Aegean Sea (see the map on p. 9). The Tenians had come under Persian control and were fighting with them (see 8.66, p. 103).

tripod   in 9.81 Herodotus tells us that one-tenth of the treasure taken from the Persians was used to set up a golden tripod at Delphi. Other offerings were also dedicated at Olympia and the Isthmus.

The battle: 8.83–95

8.83   When, finally, the Greeks believed what the Tenians were telling them, they prepared for battle. Dawn was coming up and they gathered together the marines. **Themistocles was best of all at explaining the situation.** His words set all the best things in human nature and ways against the worst. He told them to choose the better and he ended his speech by telling them to get on board their ships. And, as they were embarking, the ship from Aegina that had gone to get the sons of Aeacus arrived. At this point all the Greek ships set sail, and, at the very moment they were setting sail, the barbarians fell upon them.

8.84   All the other Greeks started to back water and were running their ships ashore but Ameinias, an Athenian from Pallene, sailed forward and rammed an enemy ship. The two ships became entangled and could not be separated, so everyone else joined battle to help Ameinias. **This is the Athenians' version of the beginning of the battle, but the Aeginetans say** that it was the ship that brought the sons of Aeacus from Aegina that started the battle. There is even a story that **the apparition of a woman** was seen and spoke in a voice that the whole army could hear. The first thing she did was to reproach them with these words, 'Gentlemen, how long do you think you're going to keep on back-paddling?'

The design of the trireme had been a matter of speculation until J. S. Morrison, an ancient historian, and Eric Coates, a naval architect, used the fragmentary evidence to construct one. Between 1985 and 1987 the Olympias *was constructed and in sea trials it has proved capable of reaching 9 knots. The trireme was the standard warship for the Greeks from the fifth century BC to the fourth century AD. Its principal weapon was a bronze ram, fixed on the prow of the ship at the water line, with which it sought to sink enemy ships.*

Themistocles was best of all at explaining the situation   it is interesting that Herodotus chooses not to have a grand set-piece speech here. It is worth considering why he made this editorial choice.

This is the Athenians' version of the beginning of the battle, but the Aeginetans say   it is not surprising that a definitive account of the battle cannot be constructed. Herodotus can only select from what he has been told by those who are bound to give their own citizens the key role. In general, he deals sympathetically with the Aeginetans.

the apparition of a woman   the Greeks are very conscious of the presence and involvement of the supernatural – see the story of Epizelos (6.117, pp. 47–8).

8.85 The **Phoenicians** were drawn up facing the Athenians – they held the wing towards Eleusis and the west – and the Ionians faced the Spartans who had the wing towards the east and the Piraeus. **A few of the Ionians followed Themistocles' orders** and didn't give of their best, but most of them did. I could list the names of many Ionian captains who captured Greek ships, but I will mention only two, Theomestor, the son of Andromas, and Phylacos, the son of Histiaeus. Both of them were from **Samos**. I have mentioned only these two for the following reasons. Because of this act Theomestor was appointed by the Persians as the tyrant of Samos and Phylacos was **named** as one of the king's official benefactors and rewarded with extensive lands. The king's benefactors are called orosangs in Persian.

8.86 That was how things were for those two, but the majority of the Persian fleet was sunk at Salamis, some by the Athenians, some by the Aeginetans. The Greeks fought in an organized and disciplined way, whereas the barbarians fought without order or intelligence, so that things were always going to turn out as they did. Nevertheless they did a much better job on this day than they did off Euboea. Everyone was fully committed and was in fear of Xerxes. Each one of them felt that the Persian king was watching him personally.

8.87 I can't tell you exactly how all of the other barbarians and Greeks fought, but I can say this story about **Artemisia** and her deeds that won her even more honour from the king. At the very moment when the king's forces had descended into chaos, Artemisia's ship was being pursued by an Athenian ship. There were allied ships ahead of her and she was at very close quarters with the enemy, so that there was no way for her to escape. So this is what she decided to do, and it worked out well for

---

Phoenicians see note on 1.1 (p. 3). The Phoenicians were the best sailors in the Persian fleet so it is ironic that Xerxes punishes them so severely in 8.90 (p. 113). See also 8.118 for the execution of Xerxes' Phoenician sea captain.

A few of the Ionians followed Themistocles' orders as the Persian fleet came towards Artemisium, Themistocles tried to play on the lack of trust between the Persians and the Ionians fighting for them by leaving messages for the Ionians at watering places encouraging them either to desert or remain neutral or not to try in the forthcoming battles. He calculated that, even if the messages didn't persuade the Ionians, it would generate mistrust of the Ionians amongst the Persians (8.22).

Samos one of the largest and most important islands of the Aegean, close to the coast of Ionia.

named in these chapters Herodotus captures some things central to the Persian way of being: the picking-out, naming and rewarding of individuals, Xerxes' desire to record everything as he had done at Doriscus (7.100, p. 74) and the Persian king's absolute power to give status to others. However, the desire to impress as individuals doesn't always lead to success.

Artemisia even here Artemisia's prowess only saves her own skin. She ends up sinking a ship from a place very close to her own city, but that event leaves open the possibility of Xerxes' pithy judgement about the effeminacy of his troops being correct.

her. Since she was being pursued by the Athenian ship she rammed an allied ship; the crew was from Calynda, and Damasithumos, their king, was on board. I can't tell you whether there had been some argument between them while still at the Hellespont, or whether what she did was premeditated or whether the Calyndian ship just happened by chance to be in the way. Anyway, **she rammed it** and sank 45 it and, through sinking it, she was lucky enough to get a double benefit. When the captain of the Athenian ship saw her ramming a barbarian ship, he assumed that Artemisia's ship was either Greek or a barbarian ship that was turning traitor and fighting on their side. So he turned away from the pursuit.

8.88   So this was one piece of good luck, to escape and not be killed. The second was 50 that she managed to get the highest regard from Xerxes by doing the wrong thing. For the story goes that the king was watching and saw her ramming the ship and one of the king's attendants said, 'My lord, did you see how well Artemisia is fighting. She has just sunk one of the enemy.' The king asked whether it really was Artemisia's ship and they said it was, recognizing the ensign on her ship. They 55 assumed that she had sunk an enemy ship. As I have said, Artemisia was lucky all along, but particularly because there were no survivors from the Calyndian ship to accuse her. The story goes that, on hearing this, Xerxes said, 'My men have become women, and my women men.' They say that these were Xerxes' words.

8.89   In this part of the battle the general Ariabignes, the son of Darius and the brother 60 of Xerxes, was killed. There were many other great men who died from the Persians and Medes and other allies, but only a few Greeks. They knew how to swim when their ships were destroyed, so that, if they weren't killed in the hand-to-hand fighting, they swam to Salamis. However, many barbarians died in the sea, because they couldn't swim. Most Persian ships were destroyed when the first 65 line of ships turned to flight. Those positioned behind them were trying to get to the front to do **something notable** before the eyes of the king, so they collided with their own ships that were in flight.

8.90   And in this chaos the following happened. Some of the Phoenicians whose ships had been destroyed came to the king and blamed the treachery of the Ionians for 70 the loss of their ships. As it turned out it wasn't the Ionians who lost their lives; the Phoenicians who had brought the charge paid the price. Just as they were saying this, a ship from **Samothrace** rammed an Athenian ship. The Athenian ship was

---

she rammed it this may be the first example in history of death by friendly fire, although Artemisia differs in doing it deliberately.

something notable whereas Xerxes believes that his presence makes people fight better, the desire to do something that he will notice turns out to be disastrous for the Persians. Perhaps the Persians are wrong for wanting to do something notable just because it's notable. The Greeks are fighting for something different and they do something notable for a greater cause.

Samothrace an island in the north of the Aegean.

sinking and an Aeginetan ship attacked and sank the ship of the Samothracians. The Samothracians were equipped with javelins so they threw them at the marines on the ship that had sunk them and swept them off. They then boarded it and took possession of it. These events saved the Ionians. For, when the king saw them doing such a great deed, he turned on the Phoenicians furiously and said it was all their fault. **He then gave the order that they should have their heads chopped off**, so that they, being cowards, should not be able to abuse their betters. Xerxes was sitting at the foot of the mountain facing Salamis called Aigaleos. When he saw any of his men performing a great deed, he asked who he was and **scribes recorded the captain's name**, his father's name and the name of his city. The presence of a Persian Ariaramnes, who was a friend to the Ionians, also contributed to the fate of the Phoenicians.

8.91 So Xerxes' men turned their attention to the Phoenicians. When the barbarians were turning in flight and sailing away towards Phaleron, the Aeginetans, waiting in the straits, performed deeds worthy of report. In this chaos the Athenians were doing great damage to the ships that were still resisting and those who were in flight, whilst the Aeginetans were doing the same to those sailing out of the straits. If anyone escaped the Athenians, they ran straight into the Aeginetans.

8.92 At this point Themistocles' ship, which was in pursuit of another ship, met the ship of Polycritus, the son of Crios, the Aeginetan. This ship had just rammed a Sidonian ship. Indeed this was the Sidonian ship that had captured the Aeginetan ship that had been acting as the advanced guard off **Sciathos**. Pytheas, the son of Ischenoos, was on board. He had been cut to pieces by the Persians and they had been so amazed by his bravery that they had kept him on board. So the ship on which Pytheas was being carried was captured along with the Persians, so that in this way he got back safely to Aegina. When Polycritus saw the Athenian ship, he recognized the ensign of the general and, shouting to Themistocles, he mocked him for **accusing the Aeginetans of being collaborators**. This was the taunt that Polycritus threw at Themistocles when he rammed the ship. The barbarians whose ships survived came to Phaleron under the protection of the land army.

He then gave the order that they should have their heads chopped off here we witness once again the random violence of Xerxes, punishing his best sailors on the basis of a single event (see also 8.118).

scribes recorded the captain's name this details fits in with other evidence about Persia and the king's method of recording good service. Perhaps Herodotus is also alluding here to the kind of sources that he used. Another thought is that Xerxes is here fulfilling the task of a historian when he should be doing great deeds.

Sciathos an island north of Artemisium.

accusing the Aeginetans of being collaborators there was always tension between the different cities because collaboration or surrender were an obvious option in this war.

8.93 In this sea battle, the Aeginetans won the greatest renown, and after them the Athenians. **Amongst individuals** it was Polycritus the Aeginetan and the 105 Athenians Eumenes of Anagurasios and Ameinias of Pallene, who chased Artemisia. If Ameinias had known that Artemisia was on board, he wouldn't have stopped before he had caught her or been caught himself. For this was the order that had been given to the Athenian captains and, in addition, there was a reward of 10,000 drachmas for anyone who captured her alive. For they were appalled 110 that a woman should be attacking Athens. As I said earlier, she escaped, and the others whose ships had survived were at Phaleron.

8.94 **The Athenians tell the story** that, right at the beginning of the battle, when the ships were engaging with each other, Adeimantus, the Corinthian general, was so struck by panic and fear that **he raised his sails to flee**. The Corinthians, seeing 115 their flagship in flight, did the same. As they were fleeing, close to the shrine of Athena Sciras on the island of Salamis, by some divine intervention a boat met them; no one could be found who had despatched it, and it came to the Corinthians when they had no idea what was happening with the fleet. For this reason they assumed that it was an act of god. When they were at close quarters 120 the men on the boat said, 'Adeimantus, by turning your ships to flight you have betrayed the Greeks. But even now they are winning a victory over their enemies that they prayed for.' Adeimantus didn't believe what was said so they spoke again, saying that they were willing to be taken as hostages and killed if the Greeks weren't clearly the victors. So Adeimantus and the rest turned round and came 125 back to the camp after it was all over. This is the story that the Athenians tell about them, but the Corinthians disagree. They believe that they were amongst the first in this sea battle and the rest of Greece bears witness to that.

Amongst individuals   one source for Herodotus would have been a record of those who won special honour, so that his account comes down to the naming of individuals.

The Athenians tell the story   it is no surprise that the Athenians should have a version of events that is violently hostile to Corinth and Adeimantus, but Plutarch is very disappointed by Herodotus' 'malicious falsehoods' (*The Malice of Herodotus* 870a). Plutarch asserts that this is not the general account of the Corinthians' performance. The Athenians allowed the Corinthians to bury their dead on Salamis, and the cenotaph at the Isthmus for those men reads:

> Balanced upon the razor's edge was Greece.
> We saved her with our lives and so found peace.

Adeimantus' own grave had the inscription:

> This grave is Adeimantus', thanks to whom
> All Greece put on the garland of freedom.

he raised his sails to flee   oars are for rowing into battle and for manoeuvring during engagement, but sails are for getting away.

8.95 As for Aristides the Athenian, the son of Lysimachus, whom I mentioned a little earlier as being the best of men, he did the following in the confusion around Salamis. He took a lot of Athenian hoplites who had been posted on the shore of the island of Salamis and put them on the island of Psyttaleia where they **slaughtered** the Persians on the island. 130

> After the defeat, Xerxes, once again, didn't know what to do, whether he should still attempt a land assault on the Peloponnese or whether he should withdraw. Mardonius proposed that Xerxes should leave a force of 300,000 Persians under his command and withdraw and, when Artemisia lent her support to this proposal, the king set out on his return to Persia (8.100–3). The Greeks, similarly, couldn't make up their minds what to do, whether to pursue Xerxes and destroy the Hellespont bridge or not. In the end Themistocles disingenuously supported the plan not to pursue Xerxes and, hoping for future favour from the king, made it known to him that he had helped him to escape (8.108–10).

1 What different sources were likely to be available for Salamis? How would they differ in their accounts? Where is such difference visible in Herodotus' narrative?

2 What aspects of the battle does Herodotus concentrate on and why? How clear an account of the actual battle does he give?

3 How does Herodotus give his narrative drama and structure?

4 In what ways do the main characters, Xerxes, Themistocles, Adeimantus and Artemisia, differ?

5 How do the Greeks and the Persians differ in this narrative?

6 What reasons for the Greek victory can be drawn from the text?

7 What does the narrative tell us about the way in which decisions are made?

8 Is Plutarch right to criticize Herodotus for being too hard on the Greeks and pro-barbarian?

9 In what ways has the previous narrative of Xerxes' invasion prepared us for this battle?

10 What is the role of the supernatural in the narrative?

11 How important are individuals in the outcome of battles and wars?

---

slaughtered   Aeschylus' *Persians* also recounts this episode (see p. 118).

Aeschylus, *The Persians* 353–477

Only one Greek tragedy on a contemporary subject survives, and that is Aeschylus' *Persians*. It is also the earliest of the Greek tragedies that survives, being performed in 472 BC, eight years after the events it describes. The play is set at Susa and the central scene is the arrival of the messenger who comes to tell Atossa, widow of Darius and mother of Xerxes, of the defeat at Salamis.

MESSENGER   My lady, some avenging spirit, some force of evil was the beginning of all our trouble. Some Greek came to us from the Athenian camp and spoke as follows to Xerxes, your son. 'When the darkness of black night descends, the Greeks will not stay, but each man rushing to the oar of his ship will save his own life in secret flight.'

As soon as he heard this, Xerxes, not recognizing the Greek's trick or the hatred of the gods, proclaimed this command to all his captains. 'Whenever the sun ceases to blaze upon the earth with its rays, and darkness takes the expanse of heaven, draw up your ships in three lines. The rest of you encircle the **island of Ajax** and guard the seaways and the sea-beaten paths. If the Greeks escape this dreadful fate and find some escape secretly by ship, it is laid down that all will lose their heads.' These were his words spoken with a confident heart, since he did not know what was to come from the gods.

The men were preparing their dinner in good order and with obedient hearts. Each sailor fastened his oar thong round the pin well fitted to the oar. When the light of the sun died and night was coming on, each lord of his oar went to his ship, and so did each commander of arms. Line called to line from their fighting-ships and they sailed forth in formation. All night long the commanders of the ships made the naval forces sail back and forth across the straits. Night was going by and the Greek army had not made any move to sail away in secret. However, when fair-shining, white-horsed day had taken hold of all the earth, then a triumphant battle cry arose in song from the Greeks, and the echo was returned from the sheer face of the island rock. Panic gripped all the barbarians who had been deceived in their plans. For the Greeks were not singing

---

island of Ajax   Ajax, the greatest Greek warrior at Troy after Achilles, was the king of Salamis.

the holy **Paean** in flight, but they were setting out to battle, confident in their courage. The trumpet blared everywhere with its cry. At once, they struck the deep sea with the regular beat of the oars together in time with the command. At once, they could all be seen clearly. The right wing first led the way, all in good order, and then the whole fleet came out to attack, and all you could hear was one great shout: 'Children of Greece. Come now. Free your country. Free your children and your wives and the temples of your ancestral gods and the tombs of your ancestors. Now, it is all to play for.'

And from our side the babble of Persian voices rose to meet it, and now was no moment for delay. At once one ship struck the **bronze prow** of another. A Greek ship started the attack and chopped off the whole stern of a Phoenician ship. Then ship rammed ship. At first the tide of the Persian fleet kept them at bay, but when the whole multitude was compressed in the narrows, none could help another. They were rammed by the bronze-mouthed prows of their own ships. They shattered all their oarage. The Greek ships, with great cunning, sailed round and round us whilst we capsized. The sea was no longer visible, so full it was of wrecks and the slaughter of men. The shores and rocks were awash with corpses. Every ship rowed off, fleeing in disarray, every ship of the whole barbarian fleet. The Greeks, with broken oars and shattered timbers, struck and carved us up like tuna or some other fish in a net. Wailing and lamentation took hold over the great expanse of the sea until the darkness of night took our sight away. Our suffering is legion, and I could not tell it all, if I told the story for ten days. Be sure of this: never in one day have such a multitude of men perished.

ATOSSA	Alas, a great sea of troubles has broken on the Persians and the whole race of the barbarians.
MESSENGER	You must know that the troubles are only half told. Such disaster has come upon us that these matters weigh twice as much.
ATOSSA	What fate could have befallen us more hostile than this? Tell me. What is the disaster that you say weighs more than these troubles?

Paean   a song sung to address a god in a variety of different contexts, for example at the beginning of a battle.

bronze prow   the greatest strength of the Greek trireme was its bronze beak with which it rammed enemy ships.

MESSENGER	All the best of the Persians in nature, the finest in character, the noblest in birth, always first in loyalty to the king himself, they are shamefully slain, suffering the most inglorious of deaths.
ATOSSA	Woe for such ruin, my friend. Tell me how they died.
MESSENGER	There is **an island**, a small one, in front of the territory of Salamis, a poor anchorage, a place where **Pan**, the lover of dance, walks the sea's edge. We sent these men there with this purpose: 'When the enemy's ships are destroyed and the men seek safety on the island, then we will easily kill the Greek forces. And we will be able to save our allies from the tracks of the sea.' So bad we were at understanding what was to come. When god gave glory to the Greeks in the sea battle, that very day they disembarked from their ships, clad in fine bronze weapons, and they encircled the whole island. There was nowhere we could turn. They pelted us with stones. Arrows fired from the bowstring fell upon us and killed us. In the end they charged in one assault and struck us and carved up the limbs of our unhappy men, until every single man had lost his life.
	Xerxes cried aloud when he saw the depths of our fate. He had a seat with a good view of all our army, set on a high hill near the sea. He tore his robes and wailed. He told his land forces to go at once in chaotic flight. This is the disaster that you must also lament.
ATOSSA	Hateful fate. How you have deceived Persian minds! My son has found in Athens a bitter vengeance. Those of us who died at Marathon were not enough. My son, who thought that he would gain recompense, has found instead a multitude of woes.

1   What points of similarity and difference are there between the account of Herodotus and the play? How might they be explained?

2   What sources might have been available to Aeschylus which were not available to Herodotus?

3   What are the key points that Aeschylus is trying to convey in this narrative?

4   Why would Aeschylus have decided to use a historical event rather than a plot taken from myth?

---

an island   Psyttaleia (see 8.76, p. 107).

Pan   see 6.105 and note, p. 40.

8 The battle of Plataea, 479 BC

After the defeat at Salamis, Xerxes was planning retreat for his army. Mardonius, however, convinced Xerxes to allow him to stay behind in Greece to make a further attempt at conquest (8.100–3). The whole of the Persian force retreated as far as Thessaly and Mardonius' force stayed there for the winter. At the beginning of spring, the Greek naval forces gathered and sailed across the Aegean to liberate the islands and the cities of Ionia. Also, Mardonius sent Alexander (see p. 80) in an attempt to win over the Athenians, an embassy that failed (8.136–44).

After this rebuttal Mardonius marched on Greece for a second time. His key allies were the Boeotians and they encouraged him to stay in Boeotia and buy Greek support (9.2). Mardonius ignored their advice and occupied, for the second time, a deserted Athens (9.3). In response to this news, the Greek cities of the Peloponnese gathered their forces at the Isthmus. Mardonius' response was to retreat to Boeotia and set about building a stronghold on the northern side of the river **Asopus**.

The banquet at Thebes: 9.15–16

9.15   While the Persians were undertaking this task, the Theban **Attaginos**, the son of Phrynon, made great preparations and invited Mardonius himself and fifty of the most important Persians to share his **hospitality**. They accepted the invitation and came along. The dinner took place in Thebes.

9.16   The rest of the story **I heard from Thersander**, a man from **Orchomenos**, indeed   5

Asopus   *not* the Asopus at Thermopylae, but a larger river rising on Mt Cithaeron and marking the boundary between Plataea and Thebes.

Attaginos   one of the leaders of the Theban oligarchy whose return was demanded by the Greeks after the battle (9.86).

hospitality   food and feasting become a key motif in Book 9: compare the Spartans' reconstruction of Mardonius' dinner and their own after the battle (9.82, pp. 141–2).

I heard from Thersander   Herodotus doesn't often name his informant. The fact that he does so may make us think that he didn't expect the story to be believed. The story is told in indirect speech, which also distances it from us.

Orchomenos   this town, situated in the north-west of Boeotia, was often a rival of Thebes for dominance in Boeotia. However, at this time it had made the same decision as Thebes and joined the Persians.

the most highly respected man in Orchomenos. Thersander said that he, too, had been invited to this dinner by Attaginos, and fifty Thebans were also invited: they didn't sit separately, but a Persian and a Theban were on each couch. When they were finished with dinner and they were drinking, a Persian, speaking in Greek, asked the man sharing his couch where he was from and Thersander replied that 10 he was from Orchomenos. Then the Persian said, 'Since we are **sharing a couch and pouring libations** together, I want to leave with you some record of my thoughts so that, having this foresight, you might be able to plan what is best for you. Do you see all these Persians who are dining here and the army that we have left at their camp by the river? You will see, before much time has passed, that of 15 all these people **few will survive.'** As he said this, the Persian **shed many tears.** Thersander was amazed and said to him, 'Should you not tell Mardonius and the Persians who are next to him in position?' His reply was, 'My friend, **what a god has decided must be**; no man can turn aside. No one wants to believe even **those who tell the truth.** Many of the Persians know this, but we follow on, bound 20 by **necessity.** This is the greatest pain for a man, **to know much but to have no power.'**

This is what I heard from Thersander of Orchomenos, and I heard this as well, that he said these things to people before the battle took place at Plataea.

The Greek force followed the Persians and took up its own position facing the Persians on the ridges at the foot of Mount Cithaeron. In the beginning, the Greeks would not come down to the plain and they were hard pressed by the Persian cavalry. However, the Megarians and the Athenians won a hard-fought skirmish against the Persians and killed their leader Masistius (9.22–5). After that, they came down onto the flatter ground even though

---

sharing a couch and pouring libations   the Greek way of dining, the symposium, had a clear ritual. Men reclined on couches to eat. In the course of the dinner libations were poured to the gods, in particular to Dionysus, the god of wine.

few will survive   this has echoes of Xerxes at the Hellespont (7.46–7, pp. 69–70), but the point is a different one. He is not referring to the brevity of human life, a common theme of poetry sung at such symposia, but to its brevity for those who are about to lose at Plataea.

shed many tears   the language of the passage has echoes of Homer (see *Odyssey* 16.191), giving it a greater poignancy and sense of tragic awareness.

what a god has decided must be, necessity   the speaker conveniently brings out one of the themes of the narrative, the inevitability of the divine will in human affairs. Such an account of causation is much more Greek than Persian.

those who tell the truth   this Persian is the last man to play the role of the tragic warner, heir to the wisdom of Solon, Artabanus and Demaratus.

to know much but to have no power   the Persian's words may make us think of all those who have offered good advice to the king to no avail.

it was not as flat as the terrain occupied by the Persians. Then for ten days neither side made a move to attack. Herodotus' explanation is that neither side could gain the right omens by divination. Modern historians offer alternatives: both sides wanted to fight on their own terrain, so that neither side would move; the Persians were waiting for Greek unity to fragment, whilst the Greeks were waiting for the Persians to be troubled by a shortage of supplies. Such motives are possible, but cannot be proved.

Herodotus also writes of the number of soldiers on both sides. The Greeks had 38,700 hoplites, the largest hoplite force ever assembled, and a total force of 110,000 (9.29–30). The Persians had, according to Herodotus, 300,000 Persians plus the Greeks who fought on their side, estimated at 50,000 (9.32). Although this is a long way from the millions of 480 BC, it is still an impossible figure. Best modern estimates suggest that Mardonius had, at most, 60,000 soldiers in his army.

Mardonius and Artabazus: 9.41–2

9.41   And so, for ten days nothing more happened. For ten days both sides had been sitting facing each other and **the Greeks had grown considerably in numbers.** **Mardonius was sick of the inactivity.** So a meeting took place between **Mardonius, the son of Gobryas, and Artabazus, the son of Pharnaces, who was one of the Persians most highly regarded by Xerxes.** As they talked about their plans, these   5 were their two opinions. Artabazus thought that the whole army should move out and withdraw as quickly as possible to the walls of Thebes, where substantial supplies of food had been provided, as well as fodder for the animals. Once they were there, they should remain inactive and achieve their ends by the following means: 'We have substantial quantities of marked and unmarked gold, and much   10 silver and cups. We should spare none of it but send it to the Greeks, especially to the leaders in each city. They will quickly surrender their freedom and we won't have to take the risks involved in battle.'

---

the Greeks had grown considerably in numbers   the Greek army was continually strengthened by soldiers coming through the passes of Cithaeron from the south.

Mardonius was sick of the inactivity   the impatience of Mardonius is critical and goes back to his eagerness for war, even after defeat in 490 BC, in his speech in 7.9 (pp. 54–5).

Mardonius, the son of Gobryas, and Artabazus, the son of Pharnaces, who was one of the Persians most highly regarded by Xerxes   this is a very formal introduction for two people who have already had substantial roles in the narrative (Artabazus was first mentioned in 7.126). The use of fathers' names and the description of Artabazus give solemnity to the moment and may remind the reader of an epic scene, for example Hector's refusal to take the advice of Polydamas in *Iliad* 18.245–312. Artabazus' father was the uncle of Darius, so that he, like Mardonius, is Xerxes' cousin. This means that he can argue openly with Mardonius, unlike everyone else.

The Thebans shared Artabazus' opinion, since he showed greater foresight than Mardonius. Mardonius' own plan was **more aggressive, more thoughtless and more uncompromising.** He thought that the Persian army was much stronger than the Greek army: 'We should attack with all speed and not allow the numbers of those now gathering to outnumber those who have already gathered. We should **disregard Hegesistratus' omens** and force them to come right. We should **follow Persian ways** and just attack.'

9.42   This was Mardonius' position and **no one spoke against him.** So he got his way. He, not Artabazus, had the authority over the army from the king. He sent for the commanders of the divisions and the generals of the Greeks who were with him and asked them whether they knew of any oracle that the Persians would be destroyed in Greece. The men who had been summoned were silent. Some of them didn't know of any oracles, others knew, but **were too frightened to speak.** So Mardonius spoke himself: 'Since you don't know anything or don't dare to speak, I'll tell you; I do know very well. There is an oracle that it is fated that Persians will come to Greece and sack the temple at Delphi and then, after that sacking, perish to a man. We know this, so **we won't go to the temple** nor try to sack it, and for this reason we won't perish. So, all of you who are on the side of the Persians should be of good cheer since **we will beat the Greeks.**'

Having said this, he gave orders for the second time that all things should be made ready and put in order so they might attack at dawn.

The Thebans shared Artabazus' opinion   the Thebans had told Mardonius before his capture of Athens that sitting tight in Boeotia waiting for the Greek opposition to unravel with the help of some bribes was the best approach (9.2).

more aggressive, more thoughtless and more uncompromising   this sums up Mardonius' approach throughout. Sometimes Herodotus tells us such things; sometimes he shows us them in the narrative.

disregard Hegesistratus' omens   Hegesistratus was a Greek diviner from Elis. He had once been imprisoned by the Spartans and had escaped from the stocks by lopping off his own foot (9.37). He is with the Persians from greed and hatred of the Spartans (9.38). Mardonius' decision to ignore Hegesistratus' omens is an act of sacrilege that will lead to his downfall.

follow Persian ways   this may refer to the rejection of Greek religious habits or it may mean that they should follow the Persian way of action.

no one spoke against him, were too frightened to speak   Artabazus, his equal in position if not in power, has had his say but now, as elsewhere in a Persian debate, there is silence.

we won't go to the temple   this is strange in that the Persians have already attacked Delphi in 480 BC (8.35–9).

we will beat the Greeks   Mardonius' words are rather empty and logically flawed. The oracle does not say that, if they don't sack Delphi, they will be successful. It says that, if they do, they won't. Herodotus does not refer to this oracle although he tells us (8.133) that Mardonius spent the winter of 480/479 consulting different oracles.

The night mission of Alexander: 9.44–5

9.44   After Mardonius' enquiry about the oracles and his words of encouragement, night fell and the night watches were being put in place. When the night was far advanced and quiet seemed to have settled on the Greek camp and almost everyone was asleep, then **Alexander, the son of Amyntas**, a general and the king of the Macedonians, rode up to the guard posts and demanded to speak with the generals. Most of the ⁵ guards stayed where they were, but some ran to the generals and said that someone had come on horseback from the Persians' camp. 'He won't reveal anything else,' they said, 'but he gives the names of the generals and says that he wants to speak with them.'

9.45   On hearing this, the generals went to the guard posts straight away. When they got ¹⁰ there, Alexander said, 'Athenians, these words are a token of my good faith. You should tell no one except **Pausanias**. If you do, you will destroy me. I wouldn't be speaking to you unless I cared deeply for the whole of Greece. For **I am a Greek by birth originally**, and I would not want to see Greece enslaved rather than free. I am telling you, therefore, that Mardonius and his army cannot obtain favourable ¹⁵ omens. Otherwise you would have been fighting long before this. Now he has decided not to bother about the omens and to join battle as day is dawning. For he is stricken with fear, I imagine, that your army is growing in numbers. So make yourselves ready for this. If Mardonius postpones his attack and doesn't join battle, stay where you are and stand firm. His **supplies** will run out in a few days. ²⁰ If this war turns out for you as you would wish, you must remember me and think of our freedom. I took this big risk for the sake of the Greeks out of goodwill. My

---

Alexander, the son of Amyntas   Alexander has already played a key role in the narrative, not least in telling the Greeks to retreat from Tempe (7.173) and trying to persuade the Athenians to come over to the Persian side after Salamis (8.136–41). Now he completes a set of pre-battle visits, Miltiades to Callimachus at Marathon (6.109, pp. 42–3), Mnesiphilos to Themistocles (8.57, p. 98) and Sicinnus to Xerxes (8.75, p. 107). Most scholars are extremely sceptical of this story, but it may be true: compare the strange story of the flight of Rudolf Hess, the deputy Führer of Hitler's Germany, to Britain in 1941. In the narrative it gives an explanation for the Greeks changing their forces round and allows Herodotus to voice the ideal of Greek nationalism.

Pausanias   Pausanias was not the Spartan king. After the death of Leonidas at Thermopylae, the next king was his son, Pleistarchus. However, he was still a child so Pausanias, his guardian and cousin, acted as regent. At this time he was likely to have been in his mid-twenties.

I am a Greek by birth originally   the kings of Macedonia claim to be the sons of Temenus, a descendant of the son of Heracles and hence a Greek. Herodotus and Thucydides accept this claim, but the Macedonian people weren't accepted as Greek people.

supplies   in 9.41 (p. 121) Artabazus says that there are lots of supplies in Thebes, but that may not be the case with the army itself.

desire was to show you Mardonius' intentions so that the barbarians would not fall upon you when you were not expecting it. I am Alexander of Macedon.'

These were Alexander's words. He then rode back to the camp and his own position. 25

Greek manoeuvres before the battle: 9.46–57

9.46 The Athenian generals went to the **right wing** and told Pausanias what they had heard from Alexander. Pausanias was **stricken with fear** of the Persians at these words. 'Since the attack is to be at dawn,' he said, 'you Athenians should face the Persians and we should face the **Boeotians** and those of the Greeks who are not facing you. This is the reason. You know the Persians and you have fought against 5 them at Marathon, whereas we have **no experience or knowledge of these men.** We have experience of the Boeotians and Thessalians. You should take up your arms and come across to this wing, and we will go to the left wing.' This was the Athenians' reply. 'Right from the start, when we saw you drawn up against the Persians, we had

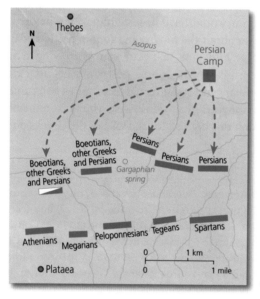

The battle of Plataea, 479 BC, original positions.

---

right wing the Spartans hold the right wing, the place of honour. The issue of the left wing had been harder to resolve in that the Athenians and the Tegeans both claimed it. After both sides had argued their case, the Athenians won it by popular acclaim (9.26–8), or so the story went.

stricken with fear it's hard to know what Pausanias thought at this moment, but an Athenian source might say this.

Boeotians Boeotia is the land immediately to the north of Attica, including the cities of Thebes and Plataea. The people of Boeotia, apart from Plataea, supported the Persians.

no experience or knowledge of these men the Spartans had been wiped out at Thermopylae, whereas the Athenians had won at Marathon.

in mind to say what you have just proposed. We were frightened that you would not take kindly to such a suggestion. **Since you have proposed it and we like the idea, we are ready to do it.'**

9.47   Both sides were happy with this and, as dawn was coming up, they were **swapping their forces.** When the Boeotians saw what they were doing, they told Mardonius and he, on hearing this, tried to change, too, leading the Persians to face the Spartans. When Pausanias found out what was going on and realized that he had been spotted, he led the Spartans back to the right wing. Mardonius did exactly the same on the left wing of his army.

9.48   When they had returned to their original positions, Mardonius sent a herald to the Spartans with this message: 'Spartans, I gather that those who live in this place say that you are the **finest of men.** They admire the fact that **you do not flee from the fight nor leave your post**: you stay where you are and kill the enemy or are killed. None of this is true. Even before we have joined battle and come to close quarters, we have seen you running away and leaving your position. You are making the Athenians take the big risk first and lining yourselves up against **our slaves.** These are not the actions of brave men. In your case, we have made a big mistake. **In accordance with your reputation** we have been waiting for you to send a herald to us to issue a challenge and to express your wish to fight only the Persians. We are ready for this, but now we find that you are saying no such thing. No, now you're sneaking off. Since you have not made this suggestion, we will. You have the reputation of being the best, so why don't you fight on behalf of the Greeks, and we'll do the same for the barbarians, matching each other **with equal numbers**? If

---

Since you have proposed it and we like the idea, we are ready to do it   a rare moment of harmony between the Greek forces who can rarely agree on anything.

swapping their forces   it may be that this story conceals some troop movements that Herodotus' sources didn't really understand.

finest of men   Mardonius' sneering attack on the Spartans tells much about his character. Herodotus' later books are much concerned with who, in the end, are the best fighters (7.9 (pp. 54–5), 7.10b (p. 56), 7.102 (p. 75), 7.209 (p. 86), 7.234).

you do not flee from the fight nor leave your post   Mardonius almost echoes Demaratus' words to Xerxes (7.104, p. 78).

our slaves   the Greeks assumed that all the subjects of the Persians were slaves. This may have been a mistake, but it polarized the difference between the 'free' Greeks and the 'slave' barbarians.

In accordance with your reputation   a reputation secured in the defeat at Thermopylae.

with equal numbers   the offer does echo one of the methods adopted by the Greeks in battle. See, for example, the battle of Thyrea between the Spartans and the Argives (1.82), in c. 546 BC. The conversation also recalls, once again, the discussion between Xerxes and Demaratus (7.103–4, pp. 75, 77–8) about how many Persians a Spartan would be willing to fight. Of course, numbers aren't the point.

you want the others to fight, too, let them fight afterwards. If, on the other hand, you think that it is enough for us to fight, then we'll fight to the finish. Whichever of us wins, that will count as a victory for the whole army.' 35

9.49   This was the herald's message. He waited for a while and, when no one gave him any response, he went back and told Mardonius what had happened. Mardonius **was delighted and, carried away by this empty victory,** he sent **his cavalry** against the Greeks. When the cavalry attacked, they did great damage to all of the Greek army with their javelins and their arrows. They were **mounted archers** and the 40 Greeks couldn't get close to them. The **Gargaphian spring,** from which the whole of the Greek army drew its water, was churned up and blocked. The Spartans were the only ones drawn up by the spring, and for all the other Greeks, it was at more of a distance depending on where they were drawn up. The **river Asopus**

This red-figure plate painted c. 520–510 BC by the artist Paseas shows an archer wearing the typical uniform of Persian mercenary troops. Unlike the Greeks, the Persians often relied heavily on archers in battle.

was delighted and, carried away by this empty victory   in Xerxes' absence, Mardonius has become the leader who has extreme, and irrational, reactions. All he has done is win a battle of words.

his cavalry, mounted archers   one of the great advantages that the Persians had over the Greeks on flat ground was the scale of their cavalry and the mounted archers who could do considerable damage to the relatively static hoplites with little risk to themselves.

Gargaphian spring, river Asopus   the identification of the geographical features is not easy or agreed, but that doesn't mean to say that Herodotus hasn't tried to give the relevant information. The Athenians were probably on the Pyrgos hill (to the west of the battlefield) and the Spartans on the Asopus ridge, so it was the other Greek forces on the flat ground who were most exposed. The river Asopus flows to the north of the Gargaphian spring towards Thebes.

was nearby, but the Persians kept them at a distance from it, so they had to use the 45
spring. They couldn't get water from the river because of the cavalry and arrows.

9.50   This was the situation: the army was being cut off from its water supply and being
hard pressed by the cavalry. So, the Greek generals went to find Pausanias on the
right wing and got together to talk about this and other matters. There were other
things, too, that were giving them even more problems than this. They had run 50
out of supplies and **their attendants**, who had been sent to the Peloponnese to get
food, had been cut off by the cavalry and couldn't get back to the camp.

9.51   After their deliberations the generals decided that, if the Persians did not make an
attack during that day, they should retreat to **the island**. This is right in front of
the city of Plataea, ten stades away from the Asopus and the Gargaphian spring, 55
where they were camped at that time. It is a sort of inland island, in that the river
that flows down from **Cithaeron** to the plain splits in half and the two streams are
apart for about three stades and then they join up again. **The local people call the
river Oeroe and they say that she is the daughter of Asopus.** Their intention was
to move to this area so that they would have an abundant source of water and so 60
that the cavalry could not do them as much damage as they could when they were
lined up face to face. They thought that the best time to make the move would
be at the second watch of the night, so the Persians should not see them setting
out and so be able to follow and harass them with their cavalry. They also decided
that, when they got to this place, where Oeroe, the daughter of Asopus, flows 65
down from Cithaeron and splits in two, they should send half of their troops to
Cithaeron during this same night to rescue their attendants who had gone for
food. For they were cut off on Cithaeron.

9.52   This was their plan and they spent the whole of the day under intense pressure
from the attacks of the cavalry. Day was coming to an end, the cavalry had 70
ceased their attacks and night was coming on. It was now the time when it had
been agreed to move. At that moment the majority of the army set out and left,
but they had no intention of going to the agreed place. When they got going,

---

their attendants   probably light-armed troops, including helots (see note on 9.80), who
accompanied the hoplites. Herodotus tells us that the true Spartan hoplite travelled with
seven attendants. The Persian cavalry had cut the Greeks off from their supplies, so they
may have been without additional provisions for three days.

the island   probably an area formed between two tributaries of the river Asopus.

Cithaeron   the mountain range that separates Boeotia from Athens. Its name has great
resonance for the Greeks since it is where Oedipus was left as a baby to die.

The local people call the river Oeroe and they say that she is the daughter of Asopus   the
Greeks often conceived of their rivers as gods and the gods as having family trees.

they were glad to run off to Plataea to get away from the cavalry and in their flight they got to the **temple of Hera**. This stands in front of Plataea, twenty stades 75 distant from the Gargaphian spring. When they got there, they set down their arms in front of the temple.

9.53   So these forces took up their position around the temple of Hera. When Pausanias saw them leaving the camp, he told the Spartans to take up their arms and follow those who had gone ahead: he assumed that they were going to the place that had 80 been agreed. At that point the rest of his officers were ready to obey Pausanias, but **Amompharetos**, the son of Poliades, who was in command of the **Pitanate company**, said that **he wasn't going to run away** from these strangers and that he was unwilling to **disgrace the name of Sparta**. Indeed, he said that he was amazed at what was going on because he hadn't been present at the **earlier discussion**. 85

---

they were glad to run off   it is a very serious allegation to suggest that all of the middle of the Greek battle-line, comprising 18,600 hoplites from 24 different states, including the Corinthians and Megarians, disobeyed orders and fled. Plutarch in *The Malice of Herodotus* (872b–c) is particularly exercised by it: 'Disobedience, desertion and treachery are the combined accusations in that passage.' Of course, such an account gives all the more credit to the Spartans and the Athenians, and Herodotus may have been led by such sources to this account. It is possible to conceive of different reasons for this retreat, but none of them have any ancient support. It is not unlikely that an army, without food, under great pressure for a day and in unknown territory, should flee at such a moment. Also, Herodotus shows, and not only here, that his account is not a simplistic glorification of the noble Greeks against the chaotic barbarians.

temple of Hera   this has not been identified. However, if it was 20 stades from Plataea, this means that they had withdrawn twice as far as they should have done.

Amompharetos   as ever, it is the story of the individual that survives. The episode may owe something to the dispute between Agamemnon and Achilles in *Iliad* 1, but it is really about bravery beyond the call of duty, or possibly just Spartan bloody-mindedness. Amompharetos died heroically and was given a special burial (see 9.55 (p. 129), 9.71 and 9.85).

Pitanate company   Thucydides (1.20.3) criticizes other Greeks for saying that such a thing exists. Pitana was one of the four original villages of Sparta and it is possible that the Spartan army was arranged on such geographical lines at this time. Sparta was an unusual city in these times because it was made out of four villages and had no city walls. Today it is a site with very little to offer in archaeological terms. Thucydides commented (1.10) that this lack of monumental building would make the city seem less than Athens to future generations, a particularly perceptive piece of foresight.

he wasn't going to run away, disgrace the name of Sparta   of course, Amompharetos' attitude contrasts starkly with the flight of the other Greeks in the previous chapter. It is also an answer to Mardonius' sarcastic response to the troop movements (9.48, p. 125).

earlier discussion   this refers to the meeting at 9.51 (p. 127).

Pausanias and **Euryanax** were deeply troubled by Amompharetos' **refusal to obey their orders**. What made it worse was that, since this was his intention, they would have to abandon the Pitanate company unless they were to give up on the plan that had been agreed with everyone else. In that case, Amompharetos himself would be **deserted and destroyed** and so would those with him. While they were thinking about all this, they kept the Spartan forces where they were and they tried to persuade him not to do this.

9.54 While the Spartans were trying to win Amompharetos over, since he was the only one of the Spartans and the Tegeans who had been left behind, the Athenians did as follows. They stayed calmly where they had been posted, knowing that **it was the Spartan way to say one thing and do another**. When the army had made its move, the Athenians sent a horseman to see if there was any sign of the Spartans getting on their way. If they had absolutely no intention of going anywhere, he was to ask Pausanias what to do.

9.55 When the herald got to the Spartans, he saw that they were still in the same place and that their commanders had fallen into an argument. Euryanax and Pausanias were urging Amompharetos not to put in jeopardy the Spartans who were the only ones staying where they were. They weren't having any success, so it degenerated into an argument and at that moment the Athenian herald arrived amongst them. In the course of the quarrel Amompharetos took up **a rock** with both hands and placed it at the feet of Pausanias. 'That's my vote for not running away from these strangers,' he said. Pausanias said that he was **mad and off his head,** and he told

90

95

100

105

Euryanax the son of Dorieus, who was the older brother of Leonidas. So he is a cousin of Pausanias who chose him to be his fellow commander (9.10).

refusal to obey their orders it is ironic that the only time a Spartan will disobey orders is when he is told to retreat.

deserted and destroyed there is considerable word play in these lines with repetition of the word for 'flight' and a play on the similarity in Greek between the words for 'desert' (*apoleipo*) and 'destroy' (*apollumi*). The confusion of the language reflects the confusion of the Spartans on the horns of a dilemma.

it was the Spartan way to say one thing and do another much of this suspicion comes from the Spartans' reluctance to leave Sparta and their attempts to disguise their intentions (see 9.7–10). It was certainly a stereotype amongst the Athenians in the fifth century that the Spartans couldn't be trusted.

a rock the Athenians voted with pebbles in the law courts and the Greek word for 'vote' derives from the word for 'pebble'. This Athenian custom is transferred to the Spartans. The anecdote takes the custom of voting and combines it with the Homeric image of heroic strength: 'And the son of Tydeus (Diomedes) took a boulder in his hand, a big thing that not two mortals of today could carry' (Homer *Iliad* 5.302–4).

mad and off his head strong language, used elsewhere of mad kings, the Persian Cambyses (3.25, 3.30) and Cleomenes (5.42).

---

the Athenian herald who was asking for the answer to the questions he had been sent to ask that he should report the present situation. He asked the Athenians to join with them and follow the Spartans' lead with regard to the retreat. 110

9.56 So the herald went back to the Athenians. As the dispute went on, dawn began to overtake them. Pausanias, who hadn't gone anywhere throughout the whole time, thought – rightly, as it turned out – that Amompharetos wouldn't really be left behind when all the other Spartans departed. So he gave the order and led everyone else through the hills, and the Tegeans followed. The Athenians, 115 following instructions, went a different way from the Spartans: they stayed close to the hills and lower slopes of Cithaeron, fearing the enemies' cavalry, but the Athenians turned down into the plain.

9.57 In the beginning Amompharetos didn't believe that Pausanias would dare to leave them behind, so he stuck to the idea that they should stay where they were and 120 not abandon their position. However, as Pausanias' forces set out, he realized that he really was leaving them behind. Therefore the company took up its arms and he led them at a steady pace towards the other formation. They had advanced about ten stades and were waiting for Amompharetos' company, which was taking up position by **the river Moloeis at a place called Argiopius.** Here there is the 125 **temple of Eleusinian Demeter.** They were waiting there for the following reason: if Amompharetos and his company had not abandoned the place where they had been positioned but had remained there, they could have gone back to help them. Just as Amompharetos' men joined up with everyone else, the barbarian cavalry fell upon them with full force. The cavalry had been doing what they had been 130 doing throughout, but when they saw that the place where the Greeks had been stationed in previous days was now deserted, they drove their horses ever onwards and, having found the enemy, they fell upon them.

Mardonius' speech and the Persian attack: 9.58–9

9.58 When Mardonius realized that the Greeks had retreated under cover of darkness and saw that the place was deserted, he summoned **Thorax of Larisa** and his

---

the river Moloeis at a place called Argiopius   this place cannot be identified.

temple of Eleusinian Demeter   a likely site for this temple has been found with the discovery of two inscriptions referring to Demeter. The temple was dedicated to Demeter as she was worshipped at Eleusis. For the Eleusinian Mysteries, see note on 8.65.

Thorax of Larisa   Mardonius and the Persian army had spent the winter in Thessaly, where Thorax and other Thessalian leaders encouraged Mardonius in his plans to re-invade Greece.

brothers, Eurypylos and Thrasydeius and said: 'Now then, **sons of Aleuas, what have you got to say for yourselves**? You can see that everywhere is deserted. **You are their neighbours** and you told me that the Spartans didn't flee from battle, 5 but were the first of men in warfare. First you saw them changing places and leaving their position. Now we can all see that during last night they ran away. They have shown once and for all, when they had to face in battle those who really are the best of men, that they are **nobodies** who have been showing off amongst other nobodies, the Greeks. You have had no experience of the Persians, so I, for 10 my part, am quite happy to pardon your mistake in praising these men of whom you knew something. However, as for **Artabazus**, I'm even more amazed that he should fear the Spartans and, in his fear, that he should express such an utterly cowardly opinion that we should break up our camp and go to the city of Thebes just so we can be besieged there. There will come a time when **the king will hear** 15 **of this from me**. There will come a time when there will be **a reckoning** of all this. But now we cannot allow these men to do this. We must pursue them until we get them and **make them pay for all the wrong that they have done to the Persians**.'

9.59   With these words, Mardonius led the Persians **at a run across the Asopus** following 20

---

sons of Aleuas, what have you got to say for yourselves   Mardonius' tone echoes that of Xerxes in his speech to Demaratus, mocking the claims of others about the Spartans (7.103, pp. 75, 77).

You are their neighbours   it's a long way in Greek terms from Thessaly to Sparta, but perhaps Mardonius is thinking in Persian terms of distance. It certainly suggests a disregard for the realities of Greece, the country about which he claims to know so much (see the debate in Persia, 7.9, pp. 54–5).

nobodies   once again, this reflects Mardonius' tone before the invasion (see 7.9, pp. 54–5). Perhaps he should have learnt something from events by now.

Artabazus   Artabazus occupies the role in Book 9 of the unheard voice of reason. Mardonius may mock Artabazus for his cowardice, but he is right.

the king will hear of this from me, a reckoning   Mardonius makes a point of his close relationship with Xerxes. Of course, there is irony here in that Xerxes will soon hear not from Mardonius, but of Mardonius and his death. There will, indeed, be a reckoning for Mardonius' hubris.

make them pay for all the wrong that they have done to the Persians   the end of the work is full of a sense that this is a moment of repayment for the past. However, Mardonius has misread the past.

at a run   this may be an echo and inversion of Marathon, where it was the Athenians who ran against the Persians (6.112, pp. 45–6). Their pace also contrasts with the stickability of Amompharetos.

across the Asopus   the moment is significant. By crossing the river he is seen to go against the omens that had told him not to engage in battle (9.37). This transgression marks the beginning of the Persian defeat.

the tracks of the Greeks who were, he thought, running away. His only target was the Spartans and the Tegeans because the hills had prevented him from seeing the Athenians' move towards the plain. When the commanders of the other barbarian forces saw that the Persians had set out in pursuit of the Greeks, they all raised the battle signals and pursued the enemy, each man as fast as he could. There was no method and no formation: they attacked, **a chaotic and shouting mob**, expecting to take the Greeks out at once.

Pausanias' message to the Athenians: 9.60

9.60   When the cavalry attacked, Pausanias sent one of his horsemen to the Athenians who said: 'Men of Athens, now is the time when we are fighting **the greatest battle of all**, for the freedom or slavery of Greece. We, the Spartans, and you, the Athenians, have been betrayed by our allies. They ran away last night. It is now resolved what we must do from now on: we must keep the enemy at bay in a way that gives us the best chance of protecting each other. If their cavalry had attacked you first, we would have come to your aid, we and the Tegeans who are with us: they have not betrayed Greece. As it is, their whole force has come upon us, so it is only right that you should come and protect that part of our forces that is under most pressure. If something has made it impossible for you to help us yourselves, **you will gain our gratitude** by sending us your archers. We are fully aware that, throughout the present war, you have been by far the most committed, so you will listen to this request, too.'

The battle: 9.61–70

9.61   On hearing this, the Athenians set out to bring help and to defend them as best they could. They were already on their way when the Greeks on the Persian side who were drawn up against them attacked so that they were no longer able to bring any assistance. They were right in their faces and this was making things very difficult. And so the Spartans and the Tegeans were all on their own. Including

---

a chaotic and shouting mob   although Herodotus has respect for the Persians themselves, he has a low regard for the other barbarian soldiers whose indiscipline is in contrast, usually, with the discipline of the Greek hoplites.

the greatest battle of all   the fame of Plataea may not match that of Salamis or Thermopylae, but here and elsewhere (9.64, p. 134) the significance of this battle is emphasized. However, such fine phrases are also used at the beginning of other battles: Marathon, Miltiades to Callimachus (6.109, p. 43), Salamis, Themistocles to the generals (8.60, p. 99).

you will gain our gratitude   Pausanias uses the language of request, not command, even though he is in absolute command. This is a very polite and respectful speech.

light-armed troops, the Spartans were about 50,000 in number, and there were about 3,000 Tegeans, who had not become detached from the Spartans. They kept on performing sacrifices with the intention of attacking Mardonius and the force he had with him. However, **they could not get any favourable omens**, and all this time many of their men were being killed and many more were being wounded. 10 The Persians had erected a barricade out of their **wicker shields** and they were firing their arrows unstintingly. So at the time when the Spartiates were under great pressure and the omens weren't coming right, Pausanias looked towards the Plataeans' temple of Hera and called upon the **goddess**, asking her not to let their hopes be in vain. 15

9.62 And whilst Pausanias was still making his appeal, **the Tegeans were the first to advance** and attack the barbarians, and, immediately after Pausanias' prayer, as the Spartans made their sacrifices, **the victims became favourable**. Now this had happened at long last, they went for the Persians and the Persians stood their ground, having dispensed with their bows. At first the battle was at the shield barricade, but 20 when that collapsed, there was fierce fighting **by the shrine of Demeter** itself. This

---

light-armed troops, the Spartans were about 50,000 in number, and there were about 3,000 Tegeans   Herodotus is repeating the numbers from 9.28–9: 5,000 Spartiates, 5,000 other Spartan hoplites, 35,000 light-armed helots and 5,000 other light-armed attendants of the non-Spartiate hoplites.

they could not get any favourable omens   no Greek army would go into battle without the correct omens from the sacrifices. The Spartans were particularly concerned with their religious duty: see their respect for festivals in the Hyacinthia (9.7, 9.11) and Carnea (7.206, 8.72, pp. 85, 106). In this situation they are waiting whilst under heavy pressure and losing casualties. It may be that Pausanias had a tactical reason for such a delay, but that doesn't mean to say that religion was irrelevant or a device.

wicker shields   the Persians do not have the heavy hoplite shield made from wood and bronze. This shield is lighter, but was not effective against the heavy weaponry of the hoplite.

goddess   the piety and respect for a local goddess contrast with the lack of regard for the divine in the behaviour of Mardonius.

the Tegeans were the first to advance   perhaps they had their own priests and victims or they couldn't stand waiting under attack any longer.

the victims became favourable   in Herodotus the gods are concerned with human affairs and they do intervene – see 8.109 for Themistocles' account of the Greek victory at Salamis: 'This is not our work, it is the work of the gods and heroes who did not want one man to rule over Asia and Europe, a man who commits acts of sacrilege and folly. He treated sacred and human things in the same way, setting fire to the statues of the gods and casting them down. He whipped the sea and cast fetters into it.'

by the shrine of Demeter   this is partly a geographical position, but it also emphasizes the divine presence.

lasted a long time until it came down to **hand-to-hand grappling**. The barbarians were taking hold of the Greeks' spears and snapping them off. The Persians were no less than their opponents in **courage and strength**, but they wore no armour, they were untrained and they were not the equals of their opponents in expertise. They 25 would dart out, one at a time, or in groups of ten, sometimes more, sometimes less, and fall upon the Spartiates and be wiped out.

9.63 Mardonius was there in person, too, fighting from a **white horse**, surrounded by the pick of the Persians, the **best thousand**, and wherever he happened to be, there they pressed hardest against the enemy. For as long as Mardonius survived, 30 the Persians held firm in their resistance and brought down many Spartans. But when he died and the forces with him fell – they were the best of his forces – at this moment all the rest turned tail and gave way to the Spartans. It was **their equipment**, the fact that they were fighting without armour, that was most damaging for them: they were light-armed troops fighting against hoplites. 35

9.64 It was at this moment that the Spartiates took their retribution from Mardonius for the death of Leonidas **according to the oracle**, and Pausanias, **the son of Cleombrotus, the son of Anaxandrides,** won **the finest victory of all known victories**. I have mentioned the names of his ancestors before this in relation to

---

hand-to-hand grappling   this represents the end of a hoplite battle where it descends into an intense face-to-face, hand-to-hand struggle after the battle lines have collided.

courage and strength   once again Herodotus presents a fair account of the battle: the Persians were not unworthy opponents of the Greeks and this was a hard-fought and long battle, as it usually is with the Persians. The key factor in close fighting was the nature of their equipment.

white horse   Mardonius' character is conveyed by his conspicuous appearance in the battle. Unlike Xerxes, he is actually at risk in the fray and he leads his men.

best thousand   Herodotus refers to Mardonius picking not only the Immortals, but also a thousand of the best cavalry (8.113).

their equipment   Herodotus describes the Persian dress in 7.61: it is very different from the heavy, predominantly metal, armour of the Greeks.

according to the oracle   in 8.114 Herodotus tells us that an oracle encouraged the Spartans to seek compensation from Xerxes for the murder of Leonidas. Xerxes' response was laughter and, pointing at Mardonius, the words, 'Here's Mardonius. He'll pay them what they deserve.' With the death of Mardonius these words are fulfilled.

the son of Cleombrotus, the son of Anaxandrides   the names once again bring a sense of the heroic to Pausanias.

the finest victory of all known victories   this is not the way that Plataea is usually seen: other battles in the war have greater prominence, especially Salamis, largely won by the Athenians. This judgement may also reflect the nobility of the Greeks' behaviour as opposed to the shameless behaviour of the Persians after Thermopylae (7.238, p. 95).

Leonidas, because they are the same for both. Mardonius died at the hands of 40
Arimnestus, a man of high renown in Sparta. After the Persian Wars, he fought
against all of the **Messenians with a force of three hundred at Stenyclerus** and
he, and the three hundred, all died.

9.65   When the Persians were put to flight by the Spartans at Plataea, they fled in chaos
to their camp and to the wooden wall they had constructed in Theban territory. 45
It is a source of wonder that not a single one of the Persians was found to have
entered the sacred precinct of Demeter or to have died there, even though the
battle took place by her sacred grove. Most of them died outside sacred ground on
unconsecrated land. My opinion, if I must express an opinion on matters of the
divine, is that **the goddess herself did not allow onto her ground men who had** 50
set fire to her shrine at Eleusis.

9.66   Such, then, was the situation of the battle to this point. Now, Artabazus, the son of
Pharnaces, had not been happy with things right from the very beginning when
Mardonius had been left behind by the king. Thereafter he had tried many times,
but to no avail, to dissuade Mardonius from joining battle. He did this because he 55
was unhappy with Mardonius' tactics. He had with him a considerable force, about
40,000 men, so, when the attack took place, **knowing full well how the battle was**
going to turn out, he led them in close order and told them all to go exactly
where he led and at whatever pace they should see him adopt. Having given such
instructions, he then pretended to lead them into battle. As he advanced along the 60
road, he saw that the Persians were already in flight. At that point he didn't keep

---

Messenians with a force of three hundred at Stenyclerus this refers to the revolt by
the Messenians against Sparta which began in 464 BC. Messenia is the territory to the
west of Sparta, conquered and enslaved by the Spartans in the seventh century BC. The
Messenians became helots, the slaves of the Spartans. In 464 they revolted and this battle
is part of the Spartan attempt to recover their control. Stenyclerus is in northern Messenia.
Three hundred seems to be a magical figure for Spartans in Herodotus.

It is a source of wonder Herodotus writes in the first sentence of his work that he is
interested in 'great and wondrous deeds'.

the goddess herself ... her shrine at Eleusis although Herodotus does not always make
such explicit statements, he emphasizes here direct divine intervention in response to the
burning of the temple at Eleusis. See 8.129, where Persians drowned at Potidaea because
of their violation of Poseidon's temple, and the fate of Artayctes for his treatment of
Protesilaus (9.116, 9.120, pp. 143, 145).

knowing full well how the battle was going to turn out in 9.41 (pp. 121–2) Artabazus
is already wiser than Mardonius and this theme is continued: Plataea is the chronicle of
a defeat foretold.

---

the same formation, but **he ran away at full speed,** not to the wooden defences or to the wall of Thebes, but to **Phocis,** with the intention of getting to the Hellespont as quickly as possible.

9.67   So these men turned and ran in this direction. Although the rest of the Greeks with   65
the king deliberately didn't try, the Boeotians' fight against the Athenians went on for a long time. **Those of the Thebans who had collaborated with the Persians** fought with no little commitment and they did do their best. The result was that 300 of their very best men died there at the hands of the Athenians. But when they, too, were routed, they fled to Thebes, although not by the same route as the Persians   70
and **the entire crowd of the other allies: they all fled without striking a blow or achieving anything.**

9.68   It is clear to me that **the fate of the barbarians depended entirely on the Persians:**
for the other troops fled at that moment even before they had engaged with the enemy just because they saw the Persians in flight. So everyone was in flight apart   75
from the cavalry, especially the Boeotian cavalry. They proved invaluable to those who were fleeing to the extent that they were always nearest to the enemy and so separated their friends, as they fled, from the Greeks. The victors were at the backs of **Xerxes' men,** chasing and slaughtering them.

9.69   As this rout was going on, the Greeks by the temple of Hera who had taken no part   80
in the battle received the news that it had taken place and that Pausanias' forces were winning. When they heard this they set out **in disarray;** the Corinthians and those with them turned round and made straight for the temple of Demeter over the ridge and the hills, whereas the Megarians and Phleiasians and those with them

---

he ran away at full speed   Artabazus' cowardice does him little credit, even if he has more sense than Mardonius. However, his actions do not seem to have done him harm: in 8.126 Herodotus says that he was highly regarded and that his reputation was enhanced by events at Plataea. Perhaps it was enhanced because his doubts were confirmed.

Phocis   a state to the north of Boeotia, i.e. on the way home for Artabazus.

Those of the Thebans who had collaborated with the Persians   this part of the battle, the fight between the Athenians and the Thebans, is much more ambivalent. There is less glory available for anyone: the Athenians are merely killing their fellow Greeks and the Thebans may fight bravely, but it's for the wrong side.

the entire crowd of the other allies … achieving anything   Herodotus is referring to the other, non-Greek allies of the Persians. Herodotus' purpose is to record great deeds, but there are none here.

the fate of the barbarians depended entirely on the Persians   here, once again, Herodotus makes an explicit statement about the reasons for the Persian defeat.

Xerxes' men   even though Xerxes is a long way away, Herodotus refers to him here, perhaps to remind us that, in the end, Xerxes is their commander and the ultimate cause of this battle.

in disarray   the Corinthians and others get a very bad press here, missing the battle and then rushing about chaotically. Indeed, the Megarians and Phleiasians perish 'ignominiously'.

went the most level way over the plain. When the Megarians and the Phleiasians 85 came close to the enemy, the Theban cavalry, whose commander was Asopodorus, the son of Timandros, saw that they were rushing on in disarray and charged them. They fell upon them and overwhelmed 600 of them and scattered the rest of them, pursuing them to Cithaeron.

9.70 So they all perished without doing anything worth recording. The Persians, 90 however, and the rest of the army fled to the **wooden wall** and climbed up onto the towers before the Spartans got there. They strengthened the wall as best they could. When the Spartans did arrive, there was very intense fighting at the wall. While the Athenians weren't there, they held their ground and were getting much the better of **the Spartans who weren't experts in siege work**. However, once the Athenians 95 did get there, a fierce and prolonged battle took place at the walls. In the end the Athenians climbed up the wall through courage and persistence and **tore it down**. The Greeks poured in through the gap. The first people inside the wall were the Tegeans and they were the ones who ransacked Mardonius' tent, taking lots of other things and, above all, **his horses' manger**, made out of solid bronze and a wonder 100 to see. Mardonius' manger was dedicated by the Tegeans in the temple of Athena Alea, but everything else they seized they took to the same place as the other Greeks. Once the wall had fallen, the barbarians no longer kept their formation and they thought no more about bravery. They had completely lost it; after all, they had been brought into total panic in a short space of time and thousands upon thousands 105 were trapped. The Greeks had such an opportunity for slaughter that of the **army of 300,000**, apart from the 40,000 who fled with Artabazus, only 3,000 survived. Of the true Spartiates the total number who died in the engagement was 91, of the Tegeans 16, of the Athenians 52.

---

wooden wall this wall brings two echoes. The first is of the fighting in *Iliad* 12 at the wall erected by the Greeks around their ships. The second is of the prophecy made to the Athenians by Delphi that they will be saved by the 'wooden walls', i.e. their fleet (7.141–3). Some believed the oracle meant a real wooden wall on the Acropolis (8.51).

the Spartans who weren't experts in siege work in 462 the Spartans were besieging the Messenians unsuccessfully and invited the Athenians to come and help them (Thucydides 1.102).

tore it down Herodotus here uses a rare word (*eripon*), which is also used by Homer (*Iliad* 12.258), thus importing an epic flavour.

his horses' manger there is constant emphasis on the wealth and luxury of the Persians, even on campaign (see 9.82, p. 141). Even the horses eat from bronze vessels. Of course, this manger would have been visible in the temple of Tegea.

army of 300,000 Herodotus is stuck with ludicrous figures: he is suggesting that they killed 257,000 in a day. 3,000 is probably right for those captured. In the same way, the figures for the Greek losses are very low, as at Marathon. However, it is not necessarily the case that they are wrong (see the note on Marathon at 6.117).

After the battle: 9.72, 76, 78–80, 82

9.72 Callicrates died away from the battle. He was **the most beautiful man** who came to join the army, not only of the Spartans but of all the Greeks of the day. When Pausanias was sacrificing, he was wounded in the side by an arrow, whilst sitting at his post. Whilst others fought, he was carried out of the battle. As he struggled against his lingering death, he kept saying to Arimnestus, a Plataean, that he was 5 happy to die for Greece, but he did regret that he had not struck a blow and that he had performed **no deed to be proud of**, despite his great desire to do so.

9.76 When the Greeks had overwhelmed the barbarians at Plataea, a **female deserter** came to them. She was a concubine of a Persian, **Pharandates, the son of Teaspes**. When she learnt that the Persians had been killed and that the Greeks were winning, 10 she dressed herself and her attendants in **plenty of gold jewellery and the finest clothes** they had with them, got down from her covered carriage and made her way to the Spartans, who were still in the midst of their **slaughter**. She already knew Pausanias' name and his origins, having heard it often before, but only when she saw him directing all these events did she recognize him. She took him by the 15

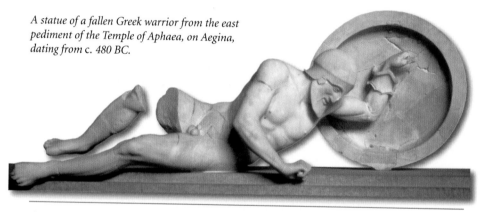

A statue of a fallen Greek warrior from the east pediment of the Temple of Aphaea, on Aegina, dating from c. *480 BC.*

the most beautiful man   this emphasis on male physical beauty is typical of the Greeks, as is evident from their sculpture and painted pottery. Compare the beginning of Plato's *Charmides* (154a), where Socrates and his friends are all excited by the arrival of Charmides, the most beautiful young man of the day.

no deed to be proud of   Callicrates is saying what a Greek should say, concerned, as they were from the time of Homer, with honour and glory. One of Herodotus' purposes in writing is to ensure that great deeds do not lose their glory (p. 2). Herodotus' narrative of Plataea ends, as does his narrative of other battles, with lists of the greatest fighters and remarkable incidents.

female deserter   the anecdote shows us something of the world of the Persian camp, a world of finery and concubines, but it also illuminates the character of Pausanias.

Pharandates, the son of Teaspes   the nephew of Darius (4.43) and a Persian commander (7.79).

plenty of gold jewellery and the finest clothes, slaughter   Herodotus draws a clear contrast between Persian wealth and Spartan savagery.

knees and said: 'King of Sparta, protect me, **a suppliant**, from a captive's slavery. You have already done great service in killing these men who have **no regard for divine powers or gods**. By birth I am from Cos, the **daughter of Hegetorides**, the son of Antagoras. A Persian took me from Cos by force and has held me in his power.'

20

'Woman,' replied Pausanias, 'don't worry. You are a suppliant and, if what you say is true and you are the daughter of Hegetorides of Cos, **he is the closest of my guest-friends** of those who live in those parts.'

Having said this, he entrusted her to one of the **ephors** who was there and afterwards, in accordance with her wishes, he sent her to Aegina.

25

9.78   In the camp at Plataea there was a man from Aegina called **Lampon**, the son of Pytheas, one of the noblest of the Aeginetans. He hurried to Pausanias with a most sacrilegious idea. Having arrived in haste, he spoke as follows. 'Son of Cleombrotus,' he said, 'you have performed a **deed that is extraordinary in scale and splendour**. God has granted that you should save Greece and thereby lay down the greatest

30

---

a suppliant   supplication was an act that had a specific ritual. The person in need of help or protection would make their plea by kneeling and grasping the knees of the person who was being asked for help. The scene recalls other acts of supplication, not least Priam supplicating Achilles in *Iliad* 24.478.

no regard for divine powers or gods   the unnamed concubine subscribes to the notion of Persian impiety (see 8.53 and 9.13 for the burning of the Acropolis of Athens and 8.36–8 for their attack on Delphi).

daughter of Hegetorides   a Greek woman of these times would not give her own name out of an appropriate sense of modesty. Herodotus' work has a number of named women, but Thucydides has only one.

he is the closest of my guest-friends   this scene has another Homeric echo: in *Iliad* 6.119–236 Glaukos and Diomedes meet on the battlefield and come to realize that they are guest-friends. They choose, therefore, not to fight each other. In the same way, Pausanias now has an additional reason to treat this suppliant with respect: she is linked to him by the ties of guest-friendship, which stretch across generations.

ephors   the five civil magistrates in Sparta and a balance to the power of the two kings. All Spartans were eligible for the office, which could be held only once and for a year. Two of the ephors accompanied the kings on campaign, which explains their presence here.

Lampon   he is not known elsewhere but he is likely to be related to another Pytheas whose athletic success was celebrated in three odes by Pindar and one by Bacchylides. This suggests that he does come from one of the noblest families in Aegina. As the work ends, there are still people offering rulers both good and bad advice. Just as Pausanias rejects this bad advice from Lampon, so Cyrus rejects the bad advice of Artembares in the final chapter (9.122, p. 146).

deed that is extraordinary in scale and splendour   so Pausanias is the right subject for Herodotus' narrative: he is truly heroic in what he has done. However, it is at such a time of prosperity that the danger of excess and disrespect for the gods is at its greatest.

glory of all the Greeks ever known. Now, in the matters that remain after this, you must act in such a way that you will have a yet greater reputation and, in future, any barbarian will take care not to undertake such acts of folly against the Greeks. When Leonidas died at Thermopylae, Mardonius and Xerxes **cut off his head** and impaled it on a stake. Pay them back in kind and you will win praise, first from all 35 the Spartans and, furthermore, from the other Greeks. **If you impale** Mardonius, you will take revenge for your uncle, Leonidas.'

Lampon thought that he would win favour from such a speech, but this was Pausanias' retort.

9.79   'My Aeginetan friend,' he said, 'I thank you for your good will and your 40 consideration, but your advice misses the mark. You raise me up on high, me and my country and my deeds, but then you cast me down to nothing, telling me to **abuse a corpse** and saying that, if I do this, I will gain a better **reputation**. That is behaviour more appropriate to barbarians than Greeks, more what barbarians do, not Greeks, and we hate them for it. So, for that reason, I would not want to please 45 an Aeginetan or anyone else who thought that way. It is enough for me to please the Spartans by doing and saying what is right. As for Leonidas, whom you tell me to revenge, I'd say that he has already been greatly revenged. He and all those others who died at Thermopylae have been paid with the countless lives of these men here. If that is what you think, don't come near me or offer me advice. Count yourself 50 lucky that you have escaped unharmed.'

9.80   When Lampon heard this, he departed. Pausanias then made a proclamation that **no one should touch the spoils**: he ordered the **helots** to gather everything together.

---

cut off his head, If you impale   see note on 7.238. As a form of punishment it represents the brutality and inhumanity of the Persians and it is, therefore, abhorrent to the Greeks.

My Aeginetan friend   there is a regular sense in Herodotus of a negativity to the people of Aegina. That is perhaps not surprising in that Aegina became Athens' greatest local rival in the fifth century BC.

I thank you for your good will and your consideration   Pausanias' restraint with Lampon might be contrasted with Xerxes' way of dealing with people.

abuse a corpse   perhaps this would remind the audience of Achilles' treatment of Hector's body in *Iliad* 22.395–404.

reputation   Pausanias, like Leonidas and any true Spartan, is conscious of his name and honour in a very heroic way.

no one should touch the spoils   once again Pausanias shows restraint and thoughtfulness in dealing with victory. However, his plans don't actually work in that the helots and the Aeginetans make a profit.

helots   the slaves of the Spartans, originally the inhabitants of Messenia, the country in the south-west corner of the Peloponnese. They were enslaved by the Spartans between the tenth and the seventh centuries BC.

They spread out throughout the camp and found tents decked in **gold and silver**, couches overlaid with gold and silver, gold mixing bowls and libation vessels and 55 other kinds of cups. They found sacks on the carts, in which there were cauldrons of gold and silver. From the corpses they stripped amulets and torques and scimitars, all gold, since they weren't bothered about the embroidered clothing. It was at this time that the helots stole a great deal and sold it to the **Aeginetans**. There was also a great deal that they had to hand over, since they could not hide 60 it all. And so it was from this moment that the great wealth of the Aeginetans first began, since they bought the gold from the helots, pretending that it was bronze.

9.82   **The story goes** that the following also took place. When Xerxes fled from Greece, he left his own tent with its furnishings for Mardonius. When Pausanias

saw Mardonius' tent, decked out in gold 65 and silver and embroidered hangings, he ordered the pastry cooks and the meat chefs to prepare a **dinner** as they would have done for Mardonius. They followed instructions and then Pausanias, seeing the gold and 70 silver couches beautifully laid out and the gold and silver tables and the splendid paraphernalia of this dinner, was astounded by all the wonders before him. He then, as

A Persian gold rhyton (drinking cup), an example of the sort of treasure enjoyed by Xerxes. It is thought that much of their treasure derived from visitors from parts of the Persian empire paying homage to their 'king of kings'. Treasuries would have been set up to store the many gold and silver artefacts presented to the king.

gold and silver   these scenes are here to bring out a central theme, the difference between the two cultures: extravagance and excess set against the simple virtue of the Greeks in general and the Spartans in particular.

Aeginetans   as with Lampon, the Aeginetans get negative coverage. Herodotus should have known that the Aeginetans' prosperity pre-dated this moment and was dependent on their involvement in long-distance trade.

The story goes   as often, Herodotus tells a story but he does not have to vouch for its authority. However, this story fits very well with the theme of the contrast between the two worlds that he is trying to explore.

dinner   the scene encapsulates the difference between Persian luxury and Spartan simplicity, but it is also an explanation of the result of the battle and the war: the Persians have gone soft (see 9.122, the last chapter of the work, p. 146).

a joke, told his own attendants to produce a **Spartan dinner**. When they had   75
prepared the feast, there was a great difference and Pausanias **laughed** and sent
for the Greek generals. When they were all gathered together, he showed them
each of the two dinners and said, 'Men of Greece, I have brought you here for a
purpose. I want to show you the folly of the Mede who, having such a way of life,
came against us who live in such poverty to steal it from us.' This, so the story   80
goes, is what Pausanias said to the Greek generals.

The end of it all: 9.116–22

> On the other side of the Aegean the Greek fleet defeated the Persian fleet in
> retreat at Mycale, a town on the mainland of Ionia facing the island of Samos
> (9.96–107). These two victories secured the freedom of the Aegean from land
> or sea invasion for many decades. However, Herodotus' narrative doesn't end
> there, but with Artayctes, a Persian who ruled the province of the Hellespont
> for Xerxes, and who was besieged by the Athenians in the town of Sestos near
> the Hellespont.

9.116   Artayctes, the **satrap** appointed by Xerxes, ruled over this province. He was a
Persian, clever and **wicked**. When Xerxes was on the march against Athens,
Artayctes tricked him by stealing from **Elaeus** the treasure that belonged

---

Spartan dinner   the Spartans were notorious for the misery of their cuisine. The males
lived in *sussitia* (army messes) and the diet was very limited: barley meal, wine, cheese
and figs. The alternative was black broth, a pig stew.

laughed   once again Pausanias' laughter is not like that of Xerxes. However, there is an
irony in this laughter. After the Persian Wars Pausanias was in command of the Greek
forces in the Aegean and, carried away by his success, went Persian, dressing as a Persian,
dining as a Persian and separating himself from the other Greeks. He thus lost the good
will of the Greek forces and ended his career in disgrace (Thucydides 1.128–35).

came against us who live in such poverty to steal it from us   this is particularly ironic in
that Mardonius had spoken with such enthusiasm to Xerxes about the riches of Greece
(7.5, p. 50).

satrap   the Persian empire was divided into provinces, called satrapies. The Persian word
'satrap' means 'protector of the kingdom'. There was a satrap for the Hellespont region
and for Ionia.

wicked   the Greek word (*atasthalos*) is common in Homer, but it is used rarely, and
significantly, by Herodotus. The Athenians use it to describe Xerxes (8.109); Otanes uses it
to describe the actions of the absolute ruler in his speech in the debate about the ruling
of Persia (3.80); Herodotus uses it of the words that the men spoke as they whipped the
Hellespont (7.35, p. 66).

Elaeus   Greek city on the European side of the Hellespont, on the southern tip of the
Chersonese. It marks the place where East and West meet.

to **Protesilaus, the son of Iphiclus.** At Elaeus by the Hellespont there is the **tomb and sanctuary** of Protesilaus, and there was here a great deal of money and gold and silver cups and bronze and clothing and other offerings. Artayctes stole all of these and Xerxes gave him permission. 5

Artayctes deceived Xerxes with the following words. 'Master,' he said, 'there is a house here that belongs to a **Greek who attacked your country** and justly paid the price of death. Give me his house, so that people might learn not to attack your land.' 10

It was easy for Artayctes to trick Xerxes into giving him the man's house with such a speech; after all, Xerxes had no suspicion of what he had in mind. When he said that Protesilaus had attacked the king's land, this was his thinking: **the Persians think that all of Asia belongs to them** and the king who, at any moment, is in 15 power. When the house was given to him, he took the treasure from Elaeus to Sestos and turned over the sanctuary to **farming**, and, whenever Artayctes came to Elaeus, **he had sex with women in the innermost shrine.** At that time he was under siege from the Athenians; he had made no preparations for a siege and he wasn't expecting the Greeks. They came upon him **entirely off his guard.** 20

9.117   The siege was still going on when autumn came and the Athenians were frustrated at being away from home and **failing to take the walls.** So they kept asking that

---

Protesilaus, the son of Iphiclus   Protesilaus led a Thessalian contingent to the Trojan War. He was the first man to land at Troy and the first to be killed (*Iliad* 2.698–702). His death can be seen to mark the start of the conflict that Herodotus here brings to a conclusion.

tomb and sanctuary   the Greeks had not only temples for their gods, but also shrines for their heroes. They believed that the great figures of the past retained power in this world, so they worshipped them at their tombs and set aside sacred ground for them. People would make offerings at such a shrine in the hope of, or in thanks for, help from the hero.

Greek who attacked your country   the idea that events from the heroic past are linked to the conflict in 480 BC takes us back to Herodotus' opening chapters and the tit-for-tat abductions (1.1–5, pp. 3–7).

the Persians think that all of Asia belongs to them   this also recalls a similar phrase in 1.4 (p. 6).

farming   among the Greeks the cultivation of sacred land was thought of as impiety and a serious offence.

he had sex with women in the innermost shrine   the Greeks thought that this was particularly sacrilegious and brought the threat of retribution.

entirely off his guard   Artayctes is presented as completely unaware that he will face retribution for his crimes.

failing to take the walls   this may seem to conflict with Herodotus' judgement about Artayctes' level of preparation. However, in the ancient world it was very hard to force a siege: without powerful weaponry, towns had to be taken by treachery or by patience.

their generals should take them back home. The generals said that they wouldn't do so before they had captured the city or the **Athenian state** had recalled them. So they had to put up with the situation. 25

9.118 Those inside the walls had now come to the most extreme of situations: they were having to boil the straps from their beds and use them as food. When they had even run out of this, the Persians, Artayctes and Oeobazus ran away under cover of darkness, climbing down the walls at the place where there was the smallest number of the enemy. When day came, the men of the Chersonese signalled from 30 their towers to the Athenians what had happened and opened the gates. The majority of the Athenians went off in pursuit of the Persians, whilst the rest took possession of the town.

9.119 As for Oeobazus, he fled to **Thrace, where the Thracians from Apsinthus** captured him and sacrificed him according to their own customs to **Pleistorus, a local god**. 35 They also killed the men with him in a different way. Those with Artayctes set out later in their flight and they were captured just beyond **Aegospotami**. They resisted for a long time, but some were killed and others were taken alive. The Greeks bound them together and brought them to Sestos, and amongst them were Artayctes and his son. 40

9.120 **The people from the Chersonese tell the story** that the following miraculous event happened to one of the guards when he was cooking some salt fish. The fish were lying in the fire and they began to leap about and wriggle just like fish that had just been caught. People gathered round and they were amazed, but Artayctes, when he saw the miracle, called the man who was cooking the fish and 45 said, '**My Athenian friend**, don't be frightened by this miracle. It isn't meant for

---

Athenian state there is a sense here of the powers of the democracy set against the absolute power of the Persian rulers. The Athenians obey their generals but their generals obey the people.

Thrace, where the Thracians from Apsinthus the Apsinthians are one of 50 tribes in Thrace, whose territory is just north of the Chersonese. Herodotus describes the Thracians as particularly savage, so human sacrifice fits in with that.

Pleistorus, a local god this may be a local name for Ares: in 5.7 Herodotus says that the Thracians only worship Ares, Dionysus and Artemis.

Aegospotami it is an irony unknown to Herodotus that in 405 BC the Athenians lost a sea battle here that was decisive in their defeat in the Peloponnesian War.

The people from the Chersonese tell the story by quoting his source Herodotus gives some local credibility to the story but doesn't have to lend his own authorial support to it.

My Athenian friend the last dialogue between a Greek and a non-Greek in the history, perhaps recalling the dialogue between Solon and Croesus at the very beginning of the work. This time it is a Persian who explains something to a Greek. The phrase is also used by Croesus at the beginning of his conversation with Solon (1.30, pp. 10–11). The repetition creates a sense of ring composition and closure.

you, it's meant for me. Protesilaus of Elaeus is telling me that, even though he is as dead as salt fish, he has the **power from the gods to punish the man who has done wrong.** This is the punishment I want to impose upon myself. In return for the money that I took from the temple, I dedicate to the god **100 talents.** In return for the survival of my son and myself, I will give the Athenians **200 talents** if I am allowed to live.'

This was his promise, but it did not persuade **Xanthippus**, the general. The people of Elaeus demanded that he should be put to death to avenge Protesilaus, and the general's own thoughts tended in this direction. So, they led him to the shore where Xerxes' bridge had yoked the straits – some say that it was the hill above the city of Madytus – and they nailed him to a plank, strung him up, and stoned his son to death before his very eyes.

9.121 When they had done this, they sailed back to Greece, taking many other valuables but, in particular, the **cables** from the bridges to dedicate them in their temples. **And nothing else happened in that year.**

---

power from the gods to punish the man who has done wrong   Artayctes sees, at last, the influence of the gods on human affairs which has been one of the forces forming Herodotus' history: actions do have their consequences and there is a repayment in this world.

100 talents, 200 talents   Artayctes is clever and is trying to use that cleverness to get off. It is typical of a Persian that he should attempt to use money to buy himself off: for him, as for Croesus and Xerxes and Pythius, money is the answer. These are massive sums of money: the Parthenon cost 469 talents.

Xanthippus   the father of Pericles (see note at 7.33). His involvement in this barbarism is worrying as the Athenians themselves turn to behaviour more appropriate to their enemy.

where Xerxes' bridge had yoked the straits   this is a very significant place, where the two worlds of East and West meet and collide. In 7.33 (p. 65) Herodotus looks forward to this moment, marking out its importance.

some say that it was the hill above the city of Madytus   the use of the alternative gives strength to Herodotus' narrative, showing that he has more than one source. Madytus, lying between Sestos and Elaeus, also overlooks the Hellespont.

they nailed him to a plank ... stoned his son to death   Pausanias rebuked Lampon for suggesting such brutality against Mardonius (9.79, p. 140) and then released Attaginos' sons (9.88). If actions have consequences, perhaps, in time, the Athenians will pay for this beyond Herodotus' narrative.

cables   these may have been dedicated by the Athenians in the stoa built at Delphi for the purpose.

And nothing else happened in that year   this could have been a strangely anticlimactic end to the work. Instead, Herodotus, as ever, ends with a story that has much to tell.

9.122   The grandfather of this Artayctes, who was strung up, was **Artembares**. He had an idea that he told the Persians and they took it to **Cyrus**. They said: 'Zeus is giving dominion to the Persians, and to you, in particular, now that you have put an end to **Astyages**. Why don't we leave this small and barren land that we inhabit and 65 occupy somewhere better? There are many lands next to ours, many further away. If we occupy one of those, we will be an even greater object of **wonder** to more people. That is the right sort of thing for rulers to do. When will there be a better time than when we are the rulers over many people and all of Asia?'

When Cyrus heard this proposal, he wasn't **impressed**. He said that they could 70 do this, but he warned them that, if they did, they should prepare no longer to be rulers, but to be ruled. '**Soft men tend to come from soft lands**. No single land can produce **remarkable** crops and men who are good in war.'

The Persians realized their mistake and left. They were convinced by his argument and chose to be rulers living in rugged country rather than, whilst living on the 75 plains, to be the **slaves of others**.

Artembares   Artembares is not known elsewhere.

Cyrus   this story takes us back to the beginning of Herodotus' work and the war between Croesus and Cyrus.

Astyages   Cyrus' defeat of Astyages, the king of the Medes, in 549 BC marked the beginning of the Persian empire (1.107–30).

wonder, impressed, remarkable   despite the different translations, each one of these words is linked to the Greek word *thauma*, meaning 'wonder'. In his first sentence Herodotus says that he will write about 'great and wondrous deeds'.

Soft men tend to come from soft lands   Cyrus' wisdom here sums up one of the key themes of Herodotus' work, the impact of the land on a people's nature. That is one of the reasons why Herodotus tells so much about places and people. In Herodotus' analysis of events, the Greeks are a hard people from a hard land and that is one of the reasons why they triumph. In the same way, Cyrus may have rejected the move from the hard lands of Persia, but, to Herodotus, the Persians did become soft, learning the luxury of Lydia. That is why Mardonius' tent with all its luxury is an important point in the narrative.

slaves of others   Herodotus' final word is about 'slavery': his history has been about the fight of the Greeks for their freedom. Herodotus and his readers would have known that the Athenians, having defeated the Persians, soon came to be rulers of others in the Athenian empire.

1. What reasons does Herodotus offer for the victory at Plataea?

2. 'No proper account of the battle can be given … it is not easy to explain the Persian defeat' (Cawkwell, see Recommended reading). Do you agree with Cawkwell's judgement?

3. How large a part does the divine play in the battle and the end of the history?

4. How are Pausanias, Artabazus and Mardonius characterized?

5. How good a military historian is Herodotus?

6. What are the echoes of Homer in the narrative? What do they add to it?

7. In what ways is the narrative of Plataea similar to and different from the other battles Herodotus has described?

8. Why is Plataea, the biggest land battle ever fought in Greece, not as famous as Marathon, Thermopylae and Salamis?

9. What are the issues raised in the final story of Artayctes and Artembares and Cyrus? Why does the work end as it does?

10. In 1.32 (p. 13) Herodotus has Solon say, 'man is all chance'. Does Herodotus' account of the Persian Wars lead us to agree? If not, why not?

Recommended reading

The best short introduction to Herodotus is **John Gould's** *Herodotus* (Weidenfeld and Nicolson, 1989). The same author's *Myth, Ritual, Memory and Exchange* (Oxford, 2001), chapters 12 on 'Give and Take in Herodotus' and 16 on 'Herodotus and Religion' are also of great value. More recent publications include *The Cambridge Companion to Herodotus*, edited by **Carolyn Dewald and John Marincola** (Cambridge University Press, 2006), which contains an outstanding collection of different articles covering all aspects of Herodotus. Chapters 1–5 of **George Cawkwell's** *The Greek Wars* (Oxford, 2006) relate to the Persian Wars, as do appendices 1, 3, 4 and 5. **J. Marincola's** *Greek Historians* (Greece and Rome series, Cambridge University Press, 2006) contains a chapter on Herodotus Book 9. Also useful for their introductions and notes are *Herodotus: Histories Book IX*, edited by **Michael A. Flowers and John Marincola** (Cambridge University Press, 2002) and *Herodotus: Histories Book VIII*, edited by **A. M. Bowie** (Cambridge University Press, 2007).

Rosalind Thomas' *Herodotus in Context* (Cambridge University Press, 2000) contains a study of Herodotus' relationship with the intellectual climate of his time; a study of the oppositions in Herodotus between the Greeks and 'the other' is contained in the *Mirror of Herodotus* by **F. Hartog** (University of California Press, 1988). *The Historical Method of Herodotus* by **D. Lateiner** (University of Toronto, 1989) is still an important work, as is **D. Fehling's** *Herodotus and his Sources*, translated from the German by **J. G. Howie** (Francis Cairns, 1990); however, I remain deeply antipathetic to Fehling's argument.

For the Persian empire, **John Curtis'** *Ancient Persia* (British Museum Press, 1989, 2006), chapter 6, has a valuable narrative together with excellent pictures of the development of the empire. *The Persian Empire from Cyrus II to Artaxerxes I: LACTOR 16*, edited by **Maria Brosius**, contains a collection of ancient sources on the developing empire. A very detailed scholarly narrative of the Persian Wars is given in **J. F. Lazenby's** *The Defence of Greece* (Aris and Phillips, 1993), whilst a more recent and very accessible narrative may be found in **Tom Holland's** *Persian Fire* (Little, Brown, 2005).

For a collection of articles, each relevant in very different ways, see *Herodotus and His World*, edited by **Peter Derow and Robert Parker** (Oxford, 2003). Chapters 1, 2, 6, 11, 14 and 18 are particularly useful. *The Greeks at War*, edited by **Philip de Souza, Waldemar Heckel and Lloyd Llewellyn-Jones** (Osprey Publishing, 2004) is a book on military history with excellent maps and illustrations. Part I is especially relevant.

The *Oxford Classical Dictionary*, 3rd edition, edited by **Simon Hornblower and Antony Spawforth** (Oxford University Press, 1996), is an invaluable reference work.

Herodotus, *The Histories*, translated by **Robin Waterfield** (Oxford World's Classics: Oxford University Press, 1998), is an easily accessible text that covers the parts of the *Histories* not translated in this book.

Ancient sources in translation

(All to be found in the Penguin Classics series unless otherwise stated.)

Early Greek Philosophy. Revised edition, translated and edited by **Jonathan Barnes** (2001)

Homer, *The Iliad*. Translated by **Martin Hammond** (1987).

Marco Polo, *The Travels*. Translated by **R. E. Latham** (1958).

Pausanias, *Guide to Greece*. Translated by **Peter Levi**, in two volumes (1971).

Pindar, *The Odes*. Translated by **C. M. Bowra** (1969).

Plato, *Early Socratic Dialogues*. Translated by **Trevor J. Saunders** (1987).

Plutarch, *Malice of Herodotus*. Translation and commentary by **A. J. Bowen** (Aris and Phillips, 1992).

Plutarch, *The Rise and Fall of Athens*. Translated by **Ian Scott-Kilvert** (1960).

Plutarch, *On Sparta*. Translated by **J. A. Talbert** (1988).

Thucydides, *History of the Peloponnesian War*. Translated by **Rex Warner** (1972) – soon to be replaced by a new translation by **Martin Hammond**.

Xenophon, *The Anabasis*. In *The Persian Expedition*. Translated by **Rex Warner** (1950).

Index of people and places